PREPARATION GUIDE FOR

INVESTIGATING BIOLOGY LABORATORY MANUAL

Ninth Edition

JUDITH GILES MORGAN

EMORY UNIVERSITY

M. ELOISE BROWN CARTER

OXFORD COLLEGE OF EMORY UNIVERSITY

 Pearson

330 Hudson Street, NY, NY 10013

Courseware Portfolio Management Specialist: Josh Frost
Courseware Director, Content Development: Ginnie Simione Jutson
Managing Producer, Science: Michael Early
Content Producer, Science: Margaret Young
Production Management and Composition: Rakhshinda Chishty/iEnergizer Aptara®, Ltd.
Rights & Permissions Manager: Ben Ferrini
Manufacturing Buyer: Stacey J. Weinberger, LSC Communications
Product Marketing Manager: Christa Pesek Palaez

ISBN-13: 978-0-13-451801-5
ISBN-10: 0-13-451801-2

ScoutAutomatedPrintCode

CONTENTS

PREFACE

This *Preparation Guide for Investigating Biology* may become your most valuable asset as you prepare laboratories for your introductory biology courses. You will appreciate that, in addition to the printed version, this preparation guide is available online at www.masteringbiology.com. Once you access Mastering Biology, go to Instructor Resources, then choose Instructor Guides for Supplements, and download the *Preparation Guide for Investigating Biology Lab Manual*, 9e.

Each year as we teach our introductory biology laboratories, we gather new ideas and suggestions for improvements in managing and executing challenging and effective labs from our colleagues, teaching assistants, and, quite often, our students. In this edition of the preparation guide, as in previous editions, we present detailed instructions, including new suggestions for preparing each lab activity.

Science educators continue to stress the importance of the laboratory component of the introductory biology course, because it is in the lab that students are finally given the opportunity to develop skills in inquiry and investigation and practice being scientists. However, for instructors and preparators, the laboratory program is the most labor-intensive component of the course. In this *Preparation Guide for Investigating Biology* we have attempted to give you the benefit of our many years of experience in laboratory preparation and teaching. Careful organization of laboratory preparation is the key ingredient for a successful laboratory program. Coordinating teaching and laboratory preparation is essential. For some, this is simple because the instructor is also the preparator, and for others these jobs include additional staff. We strongly recommend that preparators use this preparation guide along with the *Instructor's Edition of Investigating Biology*, with particular attention to the Teaching Plans at the end of each lab topic. Essential information is included in the introductory material, Order of the Lab, Classroom Management, and Lab Safety Precautions in each Teaching Plan.

In this preparation guide, each lab topic begins with a general overview of the lab activities and organization including revisions since the last edition. This overview is followed by lists of materials organized by the number of students using these items (for example, per two students) and by the particular exercise, lab study, or experiment. Additional materials are listed for the demonstration area and the instructor's bench. Separate sections list materials to be purchased from the grocery store and living plants to acquire from a greenhouse or nursery. Preparation Notes follow with additional information for constructing materials, culturing living materials, preparing solutions, and other special instructions and tips for ensuring successful experiments. We have provided References for some of the labs. The preparation information concludes with a Checklist of Materials, in which all items are again listed with a blank line preceding each item. Instructors may photocopy or download the checklist, enter the exact quantity of each item they need on the blank lines, and then take this form to specific locations to gather materials. Throughout the laboratory manual, we suggest that you project data tables for students to record their results. Many data tables are available in Excel format and can be downloaded from masteringbiology.com. Depending on the technology in your laboratory you may choose to use these with a digital projector, document camera, or overhead projector.

We have included suggested suppliers with catalog order numbers for living materials, prepared slides, and specialty items. We list the vendors, their addresses and phone numbers, and their Web and e-mail addresses separately in the Appendix at the end of the guide. Many items are available from several suppliers. We have indicated those items that are available only from one supplier. We have included a rubric to be used when grading scientific papers in the preparation instructions for Lab Topic 1 Scientific Investigation. You may photocopy or download all or portions of this as a grading aid or as a checklist for students as they write their scientific papers.

Safety notes appropriate for students in the lab are highlighted in their laboratory manual, and additional safety notes have been included in this preparation guide. At the beginning of the term, we suggest you require that laboratory preparators, students, staff, and faculty read a general introduction to lab safety and familiarize themselves with the location of safety equipment and procedures for your particular laboratory facilities. Review this information at the first laboratory preparation meeting and with students in the first laboratory period. The "Laboratory Safety: General Guidelines" printed on the inside cover of the laboratory manual will be helpful as you review safety considerations.

Advance Preparation

If you as the lab coordinator are only one person in a team of course instructors and staff, preparing the laboratory program begins as the team develops the course syllabus and schedule. The job of organizing labs is much easier if you teach both the lecture and labs, because you have complete control over the schedule. In either case, once the course syllabus is in place, determine the number and sequence of labs to be performed from *Investigating Biology*.

Use this *Preparation Guide for Investigating Biology* to plan your entire laboratory schedule. Note those laboratories that require extended preparation and try to stagger them with labs that require less preparation when possible within the constraints of the lecture schedule. For example, after the Diffusion and Osmosis (Lab Topic 3), Cellular Respiration and Fermentation (Lab Topic 5), and Photosynthesis (Lab Topic 6) labs, each of which requires extensive preparation, we suggest you have the Mitosis and Meiosis laboratory (Lab Topic 7), which requires very little preparation. The preparation-intensive genetics and molecular labs (Lab Topics 8, 9, and 10) can be followed by the population genetics lab (Lab Topic 11), which has minimum preparation. To assist you in organizing your laboratory program, here is a summary of the relative amounts of preparation required for each lab topic:

Light preparation: Lab Topics 1 (Scientific Investigation), 2 (Microscopes and Cells), 7 (Mitosis and Meiosis), 11 (Population Genetics: The Hardy-Weinberg Theorem), 16 (Bioinformatics: Molecular Phylogeny of Plants), and 28 (Ecology II: Computer Simulations of a Pond Ecosystem).

Moderate preparation: Lab Topics 13 (Protists), 14 (Plant Diversity I: Bryophytes [Nonvascular Plants] and Seedless Vascular Plants), 15 (Plant Diversity II: Seed Plants), 17 (The Kingdom Fungi), 18 (Animal Diversity I: Porifera, Cnidaria, Platyhelminthes, Mollusca, and Annelida), 19 (Animal Diversity II: Nematoda, Arthropoda, Echinodermata, Chordata), 20 (Plant Anatomy), 22 (Vertebrate Anatomy I: The Skin and Digestive System), 23 (Vertebrate Anatomy II: The Circulatory and Respiratory Systems), 24 (Vertebrate Anatomy III: The Excretory, Reproductive, and Nervous Systems), 25 (Animal Development), and 26 (Animal Behavior).

Extensive preparation: Lab Topics 3 (Diffusion and Osmosis), 4 (Enzymes), 5 (Cellular Respiration and Fermentation), 6 (Photosynthesis), 8 (Mendelian Genetics I: Fast Plants), 9 (Mendelian Genetics II: *Drosophila*), 10 (Molecular Biology), 12 (Bacteriology), 21 (Plant Growth), and 27 (Ecology I: Terrestrial Ecology).

Following our suggestions for advance planning and ordering should help lessen the stress that sometimes accompanies preparation for meaningful laboratory experiences.

Purchase a large desk calendar and enter the topics in the appropriate weeks. Use this calendar to create your weekly schedule and coordinate advance preparations and orders. Develop a dated order list for living materials that must arrive the day before or on the first day of lab. Check for the availability of plants that are to be cultured in the greenhouse or purchased from local suppliers. Geranium and *Coleus* plants used in Lab Topic 6, Photosynthesis, are usually available in nurseries in the summer but not in other seasons. We purchase these and maintain them until needed in the greenhouse, or, if necessary, order them from biological supply houses. Enter on the calendar beginning germination dates for bean seedlings to be used in Lab Topic 6, Photosynthesis, and Lab Topic 21, Plant Growth. A variety of plants are required for Lab Topics 14 and 15, Plant Diversity I and II. Bacterial and fungal cultures (Lab Topic 12 Bacteriology; Lab Topic 17 The Kingdom Fungi; and Lab Topic 7 Mitosis and Meiosis) also must be ordered in advance.

Lab Topic 8 Mendelian Genetics I: Fast Plants, is a project lab requiring 6 to 8 weeks to complete. If you plan to perform the labs in the sequence suggested in *Investigating Biology*, we suggest that your first laboratory meeting with your students be used for orientation to the entire laboratory program, for planting seeds, and for giving instructions. We suggest that this first meeting include the following activities:

- Review all safety guidelines and suggestions presented on the inside front cover of the lab manual, and show students the eyewash stations, fire extinguishers, and fire exits. Your institution may also have an online laboratory safety training program for employees and students.
- Give an overview of the entire laboratory program, describing the main objectives for the course and the writing program.
- Pass out a laboratory syllabus that includes the lab schedule, test schedule, information about how students will be evaluated, and class policies about absences and make-up labs. Review plagiarism definitions and guidelines.
- Give instructions about purchasing slides, coverslips, disposable gloves, and dissecting kits. Suggest that students may need a lab coat or an old shirt for some laboratory exercises.
- Give assignments for Lab Topic 1, Scientific Investigation. Students must have completed certain introductory activities before they come to this lab.
- Give preliminary instructions for Lab Topic 8 Mendelian Genetics I: Fast Plants. Students should then plant their seeds (see preparation guide, Lab Topic 8).

Begin expanding your fly cultures for Lab Topic 9 Mendelian Genetics II: *Drosophila*, about 3 months before the lab to ensure that you have adequate numbers of flies and flies of the appropriate generation. We suggest that you designate a separate large desk calendar to record the schedule for fly crosses and other activities associated with the lab. These flies are available only from Carolina Biological Supply. A new, heartier strain of flies is available there. Instructions for ordering these flies are presented in Lab Topic 9 of this preparation guide.

As you plan the laboratory program, determine the location and availability of other resources at your institution, including computer facilities. Will you need to reserve facilities?

Locate your field sampling sites for Lab Topic 27, Ecology I: Terrestrial Ecology, and solicit the assistance of ecologists in designing your field experience, including the identification of important species. Do you need to reserve transportation?

New in the Ninth Edition of the *Preparation Guide for Investigating Biology*

Laboratory instructors who have used previous editions of *Investigating Biology* will notice several additions and improvements in this edition of the *Preparation Guide for Investigating Biology*. The following features are new in the ninth edition.

- We have presented revised and new ideas for student-designed investigations. Many of these ideas use the same prep as the experiments in the lab topic. For some others we have provided corresponding instructions in the preparation guide, including more detailed preparation instructions.

- Most student data tables may now be found on the Mastering Biology website. If computers are available in your laboratory, you may choose to have students download those tables in Excel format. In appropriate chapters of this preparation guide, we indicate those tables that are found on www.masterbiology.com under the "Instructor's Desk" section. Once you are in Mastering Biology, choose the Instructor Resources tab, then Instructor Home, and then Instructor Guides for Supplements. In this list choose "DataTables from Investigating Biology Lab Manual, 9e."

- Lab Topic 10 Molecular Biology now includes a less hazardous stain SYBR® Safe) to visualize the DNA. We provide suggestions for inexpensive blue light transilluminators. Methylene blue continues to be an inexpensive alternative stain.

- Lab Topic 16 Bioinformatics: Molecular Phylogeny of Plants, has been updated, and photographs of the featured plants are now included in the laboratory manual. These photographs are also available on the www.masteringbiology.com website. To access these resources, select Study Area, then Lab Media. From this list choose "Investigating Biology Lab Material." You will find the nucleotide sequences and a folder with images for student use.

- Several different models of spectrophotometers are available to use in introductory biology laboratories. We include instructions for the digital Thermo Scientific Spectronic 20D+ in appropriate chapters of the laboratory manual and in Appendix C Instrumentation and Techniques. This appendix also includes instructions for using the newer model of spectrophotometer, the Thermo Scientific Spectronic 200 recommended to replace the Spectronic 20D+ and the analog Spectronic 20 that are no longer available for purchase. For the convenience of those labs still using the Spectronic 20, instructions for using this model are included in Chapter 5 of this Preparation Guide.

- Lab Topic 3 Diffusion and Osmosis has been revised to use digital calipers to measure potato cylinders, rather than vernier calipers, and the prep information in this guide has been modified to reflect this change. Figures and instructions for using a vernier caliper are now included in Appendix C Instrumentation and Techniques, in the laboratory manual.

- We continue to include lab study sequences that reflect new classifications of protists (Lab Topic 13), plants (Lab Topic 14), and invertebrates (Lab Topics 18 and 19). In addition to art, selected figures of invertebrate anatomy now include photos of dissections.

- Lab Topic 24 now includes a study of the sheep brain, with photographs of dorsal, ventral, and sagittal views, and a table to help students relate brain structure and function.

- New in this edition, we have included templates for the open-inquiry investigations in appropriate chapters following the checklist. These can be used by student teams to assist with developing their proposals. We find that the critique of proposals and preparation of materials for each team's investigation is more efficient when using this standardized format.

- Based on our experiences in lab, we continue to improve instructions and recipes in many lab topics.

- We continue to update catalog numbers and vendor addresses, telephone numbers, and e-mail Web addresses in the Appendix of this Preparation Guide.

We have tried to provide all the essential information for successful preparation of each laboratory, but experience has taught us that surprises will still occur. We recommend that you keep careful records of any failures for future preparation modifications. We welcome questions and suggestions from you, our partners in developing quality laboratory experiences. We know this *Preparation Guide for Investigating Biology* will become an invaluable tool as you prepare and implement labs that allow your students to develop their scientific skills as they investigate.

Acknowledgments

Theodosia Wade, LaTonia Taliaferro-Smith, and Nitya Jacob have been essential in giving feedback and suggestions for this edition of this *Preparation Guide for Investigating Biology*. In addition, many teaching assistants and preparators have given helpful suggestions over the years.

Judith Morgan

Eloise Carter

LAB TOPIC 1

Scientific Investigation

The first lab topic in *Investigating Biology* allows students to review and practice fundamental components of the scientific process. We find this topic is important, even for those students who have had advanced biology classes in high school. The lab topic introduces, defines, and illustrates the vocabulary used when designing experiments, and will clarify any student misinformation. Instructors will appreciate that the lab topic requires minimal preparation for the first hectic week of the laboratory program.

This lab topic features the research of Jacobus de Roode of the Biology Department of Emory University as a model of investigative process. Since the last edition of the laboratory manual, interest in Dr. de Roode's research has increased significantly and has been featured in TED Talk, "How Butterflies Self-Medicate," Jaap de Roode: https://www.ted.com/talks/jaap_de_roode_how_butterflies_self_medicate. In the 9th edition we again use the step test used in the 8th edition for Exercise 1.3, Designing an Experiment. In this exercise, students record and process data as they measure cardiovascular fitness. As in past editions, our goals for this exercise are met as students are immediately engaged in the scientific process as they design and perform an experiment using themselves as the subjects. After being introduced to scientific design in Exercises 1.1 and 1.2, students design their own experiment in Exercise 1.3 and use data generated from this experiment to practice analyzing data using tables and graphs.

Throughout the year, students will practice the concepts learned in this lab topic. Therefore, we suggest that you give instructions in scientific speaking and writing as well as experimentation. Learning about scientific writing may be accomplished in a stepwise fashion by assigning one writing activity or one section of a scientific paper for experiments performed throughout the semester. For this first lab, we suggest that you give an assignment requiring that students create a graph using some computer program (we use Excel). Use data from the experiment performed in lab, or some experiment with data that you create and hand out to the students.

Note that, throughout the laboratory manual, instructors and students can download tables used in lab topics in Excel format. Go to www.masteringbiology.com. Students select Study Area, Lab Media, Investigating Biology Lab Data Tables, 9th edition. Instructors may find the tables in Instructor Resources, Instructor Home, Instructor Guides for Supplements, and then Data Tables from Investigating Biology Lab Manual, 9e.

Grading writing assignments fairly and uniformly can be difficult, particularly if you have multiple lab sections with multiple teaching assistants. We have found that having a grading rubric for each assignment helps ensure that all papers are graded thoughtfully and equitably. At the end of the preparation instructions for this lab topic, we have included a suggested rubric for grading a complete scientific paper. You may use this for partial assignments or for grading entire papers. We give a copy of this rubric to students to use as they check over their papers, and we have an additional form that is used by the grader with point values for each item. The grader retains this copy in case a student questions his or her grade, but it is not returned to the student.

For Each Four Students

- computer with Tables 1.2 and 1.3 downloaded in Excel format from www.masteringbiology.com. Select Instructor Resources, Instructor Home, Instructor Guides for Supplements, and then Data Tables from Investigating Biology Lab Manual, 9e. Students can record their data and analyze the results.
- USB drive
- steps or platform, 8 to 14 inches high
- clock or stopwatch with seconds
- metronome
- calculator
- iPads or iPhones with metronome app (optional)

  Download metronome apps for tablets or digital phones from iTunes or Google Play. Practice with these apps before lab, and check for phone and iPad compatibility. If possible, ask your students to download the app to their phones so that they can practice before lab. Our experience with heart rate apps has been inconsistent, and we no longer recommend using an app. Measuring heart rates manually takes less time and the results are more accurate.
  Suggested app:
  Pro Metronome – Beat with sound and light. Free.

Instructor's Desk

- projection technology (computer with digital projector or document camera, or overhead projector)
- USB drive
- Tables 1.2 and 1.3 downloaded in Excel format from www.masteringbiology.com in Instructor Resources. Students can record their data and analyze the results.

  The optimum situation for teaching this laboratory is to have one computer with Tables 1.2 and 1.3 downloaded for each student team. If this is not possible, you can have one instructor's computer with these tables or use an overhead projector. Student teams can then enter their data directly for subsequent projection.

Checklist of Materials

Equipment

For each four students

_____ computer with Tables 1.2 and 1.3 downloaded in Excel format from www.masteringbiology.com.
_____ USB drive
_____ steps or platform, 8 to 14 inches high
_____ clock or stopwatch with seconds
_____ metronome

_____ calculator

_____ optional: tablets or digital phones with metronome app (see Website resources for suggestions)

Instructor's Desk

For each class

_____ projection technology (computer with digital projector or document camera, or overhead projector)

_____ USB drive

_____ Tables 1.2 and 1.3 downloaded in Excel format from www.masteringbiology.com.

_____ transparency of Table 1.3 (if computers are not available)

Evaluating Scientific Writing

General

- Follows format; all sections present and clearly labeled
- Report neat, typed, double-spaced, pages numbered
- Writing is grammatically correct
- Writing style concise, logically sound
- Title specific to the investigation; title page formatted correctly

Introduction

- Context discussed; statement of why question was addressed
- Appropriate background information presented
- Hypothesis and predictions clearly stated
- Brief description of experiments
- Reference citation in correct format (author last name, date)
- Present tense for published work, past tense for this experiment

Materials and Methods

- Description of materials, procedure, level of treatment, replicates, and experimental conditions
- Description of the types of observations, measurements, and controls
- Description of how data was analyzed
- Information on software
- Written as a narrative in past tense; not as a list or steps
- Level of detail for repeating work; not unimportant details

Results

- Results reported accurately (results observed, not what was expected)
- Tables, graphs, drawings of high quality; clear labels, titles, consecutively numbered
- Data presented and analyzed appropriately (e.g., chi square, mean, averages, percent differences, etc.)
- Summary of results in paragraph form with reference to all tables and figures
- Trends and patterns emphasized and supported with data
- Statements supported with reference to data
- Methods, meaning of results, interpretation are not included
- Concise and clearly written

Discussion

- Brief summary of experiment, stating hypotheses and predictions
- Interpretation of data; clear explanation with reference to results
- Data related to the question or hypothesis; supports or negates
- Significance of results discussed, related to previous work or outside sources
- References included and properly cited in text
- Conclusions drawn and supported by data
- Weaknesses stated briefly if results affected, but not overdone

Acknowledgments

- Names of teammates and others along with their contributions

References Cited

- All references in text are in References Cited section (and vice versa)
- References appropriate to project
- References meet instructor's requirement for number and type
- Format correct

Abstract

- One paragraph, fewer than 250 words
- Clear statement of question and hypothesis
- Summary of methods (3–4 sentences)
- Summary of major results (2–3 sentences)
- Concluding statement relating results to hypothesis

Microscopes and Cells

Many supplies will be available at each student's work station; however, students will also share a variety of materials in this lab. Have these shared supplies available at a central location, arranged in the order of the laboratory, and clearly labeled with the name of the organism (or material) and the corresponding exercise number.

Note that we continue to follow the latest literature that designates *Volvox* as a multicellular organism rather than a colonial organism as in some texts. Multicellular organisms are defined as those with two or more types of cells with specialized structure and function, and these cell types, when isolated, are not capable of perpetuating the species. The latest studies of *Volvox* have confirmed that these criteria are true for this organism.

Reference materials may be available online or as printed materials in the laboratory. If computers with Web access are available in the laboratory, locate suggested sites describing electron microscopy before lab begins (see Lab Topic 2 in the lab manual). If you plan to use a video (see Reference Materials) for describing the electron microscope, schedule the appropriate audiovisual equipment for this laboratory.

Laboratory instructors may find it helpful to have a photomicroscopy system available to assist students in locating and orienting structures as they study microscope slides. Take care, however, that students do not rely on projected images rather than observing their own slides. In addition to improving microscope skills, searching a slide and observing variations in slides are valuable exercises.

In this edition of *Investigating Biology*, we added a new suggestion for an investigative extension where students use Web resources to review the use and design of the inverted microscope, the fluorescent microscope, and the confocal microscope. If these microscopes are available in your department, as an investigative extension a student could compare images of tissues of their choice as viewed with the compound light microscope and each of these microscopes.

For Each Student

- compound microscope
- dissecting (stereoscopic) microscope (These may be shared.)
- lens paper (Carolina Biological Supply # 634000)
- microscope slides and glass coverslips (We have students supply their own.)
- pond water culture, Exercise 2.5, Lab Study D (Each student should collect his or her own. Provide Pasteur pipettes and bulbs or transfer pipettes.)

Exercise 2.2

- thin, clear plastic 15-cm ruler
- letter slide (Carolina Biological Supply # 291406)
- crossed-thread slide (Carolina Biological Supply # 291418)

For Each Two Students

- dissecting needles (Carolina Biological Supply # 627220)
- forceps (Carolina Biological Supply # 624084)
- flat toothpicks in petri dish, Exercise 2.5, Lab Study C
- small petri dish with sand grains or glass chips from broken coverslips, Exercise 2.5, Lab Study C
- Kimwipes™ (Carolina Biological Supply # 633950)
- squirt bottle of deionized (DI) water (may share with another group)
- dropper bottles of:
  deionized (DI) water (Distilled water can be substituted.)
  Insect Ringer's solution, Exercise 2.5, Lab Study A
  0.1% methylene blue, Exercise 2.5, Lab Study C

Demonstration/Supplies Table

Materials should be set up in a demonstration area so that they follow the sequence of the lab. Clearly label each area with the number of the exercise, the organism or cell structure, and so on, that is to be seen. For living cultures, include a note reminding students not to exchange pipettes among the living cultures.

- electron micrographs for student observations
  Excellent images are provided for instructors with the textbook and can be projected or used as a bulletin board display. Micrographs are also available from several websites. Print these to display on a bulletin board.
- resource materials on the use of the electron microscope
  See websites listed in the lab topic. Also, doing an online search provides several websites.
- living cultures each with Pasteur pipette and bulb:
  Amoeba under dissecting scope (Carolina Biological Supply # 131306)
  Scenedesmus (Carolina Biological Supply # 152510)
  Volvox (Carolina Biological Supply # 152665)
  Elodea (Carolina Biological Supply # 157340, or pet stores, aquarium plant)
  unknowns if students did not bring pond water
- other cultures:
  termites with forceps
  Protococcus growing on tree bark with forceps and dissecting needles
- 2 containers of 10% household bleach (final dilution = 0.6% sodium hypochlorite), one for disposal of used toothpicks, the other for cheek-cell slides

Instructor's Desk

- projection technology (computer with digital projector or document camera, or overhead projector)
- reference books for pond water unknowns
- references for electron microscopy
- photomicroscopy system (optional)

Solution Preparation Notes

0.1% Methylene Blue

Dissolve 1 g in 1000 mL of DI water.

Insect Ringer's Solution

This is a saline solution that is isotonic to the internal environment of insects. The solution is 0.75% saline. Dissolve 7.5 g NaCl in 1000 mL of DI water.

Live/Prepared Materials

Cultures can be ordered from biological supply houses. The *Amoeba* and *Volvox* do not live for extended periods. Consider scheduling the arrival of fresh materials if these will be used more than 2 days.

Students usually have difficulty locating *Amoeba* on their slides. To improve their chances of having several on the slide, we recommend that you prepare the slides before the activity begins. If you do this, or if students make their own slides, we suggest that you follow this procedure:

> Allow the culture to settle undisturbed for 30 minutes. Pipette off about ¾ of the liquid into a clean container (this liquid may contain amoebae). Carefully move the culture dish to a dissecting microscope and focus on the bottom of the container. You should be able to see the amoebae. Squeeze the transfer pipette bulb supplied with the culture, insert it to the bottom of the dish, and pull up a drop of liquid. Place one small drop of this liquid on each slide. Apply a coverslip carefully. You may be able to make several slides from this one attempt. If you have time, using the highest magnification on the dissecting microscope, scan the slide to locate the amoebae before passing it out to students. Students can use this same procedure. Since they are just learning how to use the compound microscope, they may not be focusing in the correct plane on the slide. Have them first focus on the edge of the coverslip, and then scan the slide for an amoeba.

Protococcus

Collect these from pine trees in the area (if available). *Protococcus* grows best on the northern face of the tree, usually less than a meter above the ground. It appears as a bright greenish film within cracks and grooves of the bark. A grayish-green lichen is often mixed with *Protococcus.* One can easily distinguish the two by color. With a pocketknife or scalpel, cut or peel off small sections of the bark with *Protococcus.* Place in small petri dishes or finger bowls. *Protococcus* will survive on the shelf in jars for several months. Cultures are also available from biological suppliers (Carolina Biological Supply # 151310).

Termites

Cultures can be ordered from biological supply houses (Carolina Biological Supply # 143738) or collected from rotting wood. Check the termite gut to be sure flagellates are alive. They require a food source (wood) and should be maintained in a moist environment in the lab. Protozoans that are present but not actively moving can be used in lab, but the student response is less dramatic.

Pond Water/Unknowns for Exercise 2.5, Lab Study D

The best source of organisms for this study is a convenient pond. Students or the instructor can collect these samples using a plankton net or just a jar. In addition, consider submerging microscope slides into the pond for several days before the lab. We have prepared collecting boxes by cutting large squares out of the flat sides of old plastic slide boxes. Insert slides into the box and wire it closed. Then suspend the box under the water surface. Sessile organisms will attach to the slides. Students must then wipe one side of the slide clean before they place it on the microscope stage. View this first without, and then with, a coverslip.

If a pond is not available, you can order protozoan and algae survey mixtures (Carolina Biological Supply # 151216 and # 132060). Survey mixtures often come with a key to organisms. Another alternative is a "Hay Infusion Kit" for culturing microorganisms (Carolina Biological Supply # 131206), or you can make your own with hay from a feed store (usually free). To maintain your kit all semester, add used microorganism cultures, hay, and water as needed.

Reference Materials

If the instructor plans to use a video on electron microscopy, schedule the appropriate audiovisual equipment for the laboratory. If computers are available in the laboratory, choose websites to show the use of the transmission electron microscope.

Electron Micrographs

Images of electron micrographs are supplied to instructors with most textbooks. These may be posted on a bulletin board.

Try an online search for electron micrograph images.

Excellent plant cell micrographs produced by Edon Newcomb at the University of Wisconsin may be printed and displayed. http://botit.botany.wisc.edu/Resources/electron micrographs.

Good micrographs of organelles in animal cells are available at https://www.uni-mainz.de/FB/ Medizin/Anatomie/workshop/EM/EMRERE.html.

Other electron micrographs of many cells are available at http://www.bu.edu/histology/m/t_electr.htm.

Electron Microscope Procedures

Bozzola, J. J., and L. D. Russell. 1992. *Electron Microscopy,* 2nd ed. Sudbury, MA: Jones and Bartlett Publishers.

Hayat, M. A. 2000. *Principles and Techniques of Electron Microscopy,* 4th ed. New York: Cambridge University Press.

To locate information about the transmission electron microscope, search the phrase "electron microscope structure and function." One excellent video is found at this site: http://www.youtube.com/watch?v=fToTFjwUc5M See also "Scanning Electron Microscope," "Images from a Scanning Electron Microscope," and "Amazing Scanning Electron Microscope."

Freshwater Plankton

Palmer, C. Mervin. 1962. *Algae in Water Supplies.* Public Health Service Publication No. 657. Washington, D.C.: U.S. Dept. of Health, Education and Welfare, Public Health Service.

Wehr, J. D., and R. G. Sheath, eds. 2003. *Freshwater Algae of North America.* San Diego: Elsevier Science (USA).

Information on collecting and identifying organisms found in a freshwater pond: http://www.microscopy-uk.org.uk/pond/index.html

Checklist of Materials

Equipment

For each student

_____ compound microscope (1)
_____ stereoscopic (dissecting) microscope (1)
_____ lens paper (1 pack)
_____ clear plastic ruler (1)
_____ microscope slides (1 box)
_____ glass coverslips (1 box)

For each two students

_____ forceps (1)
_____ dissecting needle (1)
_____ small petri dish with glass chips or sand (1)
_____ flat toothpicks in petri dish (1 dish with 2)
_____ Pasteur pipette and bulb (1)
_____ Kimwipes (1)
_____ squirt bottle of DI water (1)

Demonstration/Supplies Table

For each class

_____ electron micrographs (1 set)
_____ resource materials on the electron microscope
living cultures each with Pasteur pipette and bulb or transfer pipette:
_____ *Amoeba* under dissecting scope
_____ *Scenedesmus*
_____ *Volvox*
_____ *Elodea*
_____ unknowns if students did not bring pond water
other cultures:
_____ termites with forceps
_____ *Protococcus* with forceps and dissecting needles
_____ containers of disinfectant (2)

Instructor's Desk

For each class

_____ projection technology (computer with digital projector or document camera, or overhead projector)
_____ reference books, printed or electronic information for pond water unknowns
_____ reference books, printed or electronic information for electron microscopy
_____ reference video for electron microscopy (optional)
_____ photomicroscopy system (optional)

Solutions/Chemicals

For each two students

dropper bottles of:
_____ 0.1% methylene blue (1)
_____ Insect Ringer's solution (1)
_____ DI water (1)

Live/Prepared Materials

For each student

prepared slides of:
_____ crossed threads (1)
_____ letter (1)

Diffusion and Osmosis

Lab Topic 3 allows students to perform many interesting investigations that will improve their understanding of several very important biological concepts. With careful planning, all experiments are easily completed in a 3-hour lab period (see Teaching Plan). To save time, you may do Exercise 3.1, Lab Study A, Kinetic Energy of Molecules, as a demonstration using a photomicroscopy system or, if computers are available, do an online search for: Video, Brownian Movement. YouTube "Nano particles in water" is a good example. Note that two other experiments are also demonstrations: Exercise 3.2, Experiment A (Procedure step 1 — red blood cells in test tubes) and Experiment B, the *Elodea* experiment. Another possible demonstration is described in a marginal note with Exercise 3.2, Experiment B, and uses a carrot or a celery petiole in distilled water and concentrated salt solution.

As written, students work independently as they observe Brownian movement (Exercise 3.1, Lab Study A) and red blood cells in different molar solutions (Exercise 3.2, Experiment A). Experiments investigating potato osmolarity (Exercise 3.3) are performed in teams of four, with some teams investigating change in weight (Experiment A) and others investigating change in volume (Experiment B). In a class of 24 students, we have three teams investigating weight change and three teams investigating volume change in the potato pieces.

For Each Student

- compound microscope, Exercise 3.1, Lab Study A; Exercise 3.2, Experiment A
- slides and coverslips, Exercise 3.1, Lab Study A; Exercise 3.2, Experiment A (We ask students to supply their own.)

For Each Four Students

- computer with Tables 3.5 and 3.6 downloaded in Excel format from www.masteringbiology.com. Students select Study Area, Lab Media, Investigating Biology Lab Data Tables — 9th edition. Instructors, select Instructor Resources. In Instructor Home select Instructor Guides for Supplements, and then Data Tables from Investigating Biology Lab Manual, 9e. Students can record their data and analyze the results.
- USB drive

Place on lab bench in student work area:
- hot plate
- 500-mL beaker one-third filled with water for Benedict's test (Place this beaker on the hot plate.)

Dispense the remaining student supplies on cafeteria trays, one tray for four students. Label half the trays "volume," the other half "weight."

Exercise 3.1, Experiment A

- dropper bottle of water
- small container of carmine powder
- 2 dissecting needles

Exercise 3.1, Experiment B

- 3 standard test tubes (16 mm × 150 mm)
- wax pencil
- 2 handheld test-tube holders
- 5¼-in. disposable plastic transfer pipettes (Pasteur pipettes may be used, but they must be used carefully to avoid piercing the dialysis bag.)
- small balloon-type bulbs if you use Pasteur pipettes
- dry 400-mL beaker to hold the dialysis bag after the experiment
- small piece of string or rubber band to close end of dialysis tubing (We prefer to use small rubber bands.)
- 30-cm strip of 1-in.-wide dialysis tubing (Carolina Biological Supply # 684216)

    Place this in a 400-mL beaker filled with about 200 mL DI water on the tray. The water makes the tubing easier to manipulate, and the beaker can then be used for the experiment.

- approximately 10 mL 30% glucose solution in a small beaker
- approximately 10 mL 1% starch solution in a small beaker
- small dark bottles of concentrated I_2KI solution (Dropper bottles may be sufficient.)
- dropper bottle of Benedict's solution
- flask of DI water (for control)

Exercise 3.2, Experiment A

- oxen blood in small bottle with 5¼-in. disposable Pasteur pipette and bulb
- 125-mL flasks labeled "A," "B," and "C" with the following solutions:

    A = DI water, the hypotonic solution

    B = 0.154 M NaCl, the isotonic solution

    C = concentrated NaCl, the hypertonic solution

    Each flask should have a disposable pipette with bulb or a transfer pipette.

- beaker with 10% bleach for discarded blood slides (optional)

Exercise 3.3, Experiments A and B

- paper towels
- large potato tuber
- 7 250-mL beakers or 9-oz disposable, stackable plastic cups (We use plastic cups and reuse them indefinitely.)
- forceps
- 6-mm cork borer (You need a punch to push out the potato core. We use handles of bacterial transfer loops.)
- 15-cm metric ruler
- 10-cm squares of aluminum foil to hold the potato pieces (Disposable plastic weighing dishes work better but are more expensive.)
- single-edge razor blade

- petri dish with lid
- digital caliper or vernier caliper (on the *volume* trays only): vernier caliper (Carolina Biological Supply # 702651); metric vernier dial caliper (Carolina Biological Supply # 702662); digital caliper (Fowler 6″ Poly-Cal Electronic Caliper # 541011750. Check for distributors online at www.fowlerprecision.com)

Demonstration/Supplies Table

Exercise 3.2, Experiment A

- test-tube rack
- 3 test tubes with screw caps labeled "A," "B," or "C," each containing one of the three solutions of unknown osmolarity.
  Solution A = DI water
  Solution B = 0.154 *M* NaCl
  Solution C = concentrated NaCl

  (Vary as you choose, but use the same solutions as in the microscopic observations.) Add 5 drops of ox blood to each tube.
- printed page

Exercise 3.2, Experiment B

- 2 compound microscopes labeled "A" and "B"
- 2 slides of living *Elodea:* 1 in DI or distilled water, 1 in a concentrated NaCl solution

  Seal these slides with petroleum jelly to prevent drying out during the lab. Use a toothpick to apply the jelly to the edges of the coverslip.

Exercise 3.2, Experiment B: Optional Demonstration

- 2 beakers, one labeled "A," the other "B," placed beside the corresponding microscope
- respective solutions in beakers
- carrot or celery petiole in each beaker
- paper towels

Exercise 3.3

- 7 1-L flasks, each labeled and filled with one of the following solutions:
  DI water, 0.1 *M* sucrose, 0.2 *M* sucrose, 0.3 *M* sucrose, 0.4 *M* sucrose, 0.5 *M* sucrose, 0.6 *M* sucrose

  Students must measure 100 mL of each of the solutions. To facilitate this, use 150–250-mL beakers with approximate graduations, one labeled for each solution. Place each beaker beside the appropriate solution on the supplies table.
- balance that weighs to the nearest 0.01 g (One balance is adequate—two are better.)

Instructor's Desk

- projection technology (computer with digital projector or document camera, or overhead projector)

- Tables 3.5 and 3.6 downloaded in Excel format from www.masteringbiology.com in Instructor Resources. Students can record their data, and then analyze and share their results.
- USB drive
- overhead projector (if computers are not available)
- washable pens
- blank transparencies or transparencies of Table 3.5 and Table 3.6 (if computers are not available)
- photomicroscopy system (optional)

Grocery Supplies

- granulated (table) sugar (about 1.5 1b per lab of 24 students) (Use this for the sucrose solutions.)
- baking potatoes (1 per four students) (We buy them by the case at the farmers' market.)
- 9-oz disposable cups (7 per four students)

Solution Preparation Notes

Oxen Blood

Purchase oxen blood (Carolina Biological Supply # 828570 citrated). Sheep's blood can be substituted (Carolina Biological Supply # 828950 citrated). It also can be purchased from Cleveland Scientific. Do not use human blood. Keep blood stocks refrigerated. On the day of the lab, dispense into small containers, about 5 mL in each, cover, and refrigerate until lab time.

Before dispensing, use a microscope to check the blood, as it sometimes arrives already crenated. If the blood is crenated, tell students to note this in their lab manuals before beginning the experiment. The blood cells will still respond to the solutions as expected. They will swell and burst in the hypotonic solution, they may return to normal in the isotonic solution, and they may become more crenated in the hypertonic solution.

Sucrose Solutions

For a lab of 24 students, you will need about 600 mL of each concentration. We make 4–5 L of each and keep it refrigerated. Replenish the lab room's stocks when needed. Be prepared for the mess—the demonstration table will become very sticky. You can use table sugar purchased at a grocery for these solutions.

For 1000 mL of each solution, weigh the following amounts of sugar and add DI water up to 1000 mL:

$$0.1\ M = 34.2\ \text{g}$$
$$0.2\ M = 68.4\ \text{g}$$
$$0.3\ M = 102.6\ \text{g}$$
$$0.4\ M = 136.8\ \text{g}$$
$$0.5\ M = 171.0\ \text{g}$$
$$0.6\ M = 205.2\ \text{g}$$

0.154 *M* NaCl

For 1000 mL, weigh 9.02 g of NaCl and add DI water up to 1000 mL.

Benedict's Solution

This can be purchased already mixed from a biological supply house. However, it is easy to make, and it keeps well for long periods of time.

To make 1 L:

1. Add 173 g sodium citrate (Carolina Biological Supply # 889060) and 100 g anhydrous sodium carbonate (Carolina Biological Supply # 888770) to 600 mL of DI water. Heat and stir until dissolved.
2. Filter.
3. Add 17.3 g copper sulfate (Carolina Biological Supply # 856589) to 150 mL DI water. Stir until dissolved.
4. Slowly add the copper sulfate solution to the sodium citrate and sodium carbonate solution, stirring constantly.
5. Add DI water to bring the total volume to 1000 mL.

Glucose Test Strips

One reviewer suggested replacing Benedict's Solution with glucose test strips (Carolina Biological Supply # 893840). Because we have never used these we recommend that you try this experiment with test strips before introducing this procedure to your students. However, there is some value to using the Benedict's test, as students learn laboratory skills, and it is exciting to see the solutions change colors.

I_2KI

To make 1000 mL:

1. Dissolve 20 g of potassium iodide (KI) (Carolina Biological Supply # 883789) in 1000 mL DI water. Dissolve 10 g of iodine (Carolina Biological Supply # 868982) in the KI solution.
2. Store this stock solution in a large dark bottle. I_2KI solutions break down in light. The day of lab, pour some of the stock into a beaker and dispense into the students' dropper bottles. We collect all I_2KI droppers at the end of the lab and store them in the dark until they are used again.

1% Starch Solution

Note that you will need approximately 10 mL of solution per group of four students.

1. Add 1 g potato starch (Sigma # S 4251) to 100 mL DI water.
2. Heat and stir with a magnetic stirrer until the solution just boils. The starch must completely dissolve. The solution will turn from opaque to slightly translucent, a "glowing" appearance.
3. Remove from the heat to prevent scorching. Test a drop of starch with a drop of I_2KI. If the starch has heated long enough and is in solution, the drop will turn purple-black.

30% Glucose

Note that you will need approximately 10 mL of solution per group of four students. Add 30 g glucose (Sigma # G 8270) to 100 mL DI water. Stir and heat if necessary.

Investigative Extensions

Living marine invertebrates for salinity tolerance investigations may be purchased from Gulf Speciman and Woods Hole Marine Biological Laboratory. See the appendix for contact information.

Checklist of Materials

Equipment

For each student

_____ compound microscope (1)
_____ slides (4–6)
_____ glass coverslips (4–6)

For each four students

_____ computer with Tables 3.5 and 3.6 downloaded in Excel format from www.masteringbiology.com
_____ USB drive
_____ dissecting needles (2)
_____ wax pencils (2)
_____ handheld test-tube holders (2)
_____ plastic transfer pipettes or Pasteur pipettes (2–4)
_____ small bulbs for Pasteur pipettes (2–4)
_____ 30-cm strip of 1-in. dialysis tubing (1)
_____ string or rubber band (1)
_____ paper towels (1 stack)
_____ potato (1)
_____ forceps (2)
_____ cork borer with a punch (1)
_____ 15-cm metric ruler (1)
_____ 10-cm square of aluminum foil (1)
_____ single-edge razor blades (2)
_____ hot plate (1)
_____ tray (1)

For each class

_____ vernier calipers (3 per class of 24), Exercise 3.3, Experiment B

Glassware

For each four students

_____ standard test tubes (16 × 150 mm) (3)
_____ 5¼-in. disposable Pasteur pipettes (5)
_____ 400-mL beakers (2)
_____ 500-mL beaker (1)
_____ 250-mL beakers or 9-oz plastic cups (7)
_____ petri dish with lid (1)
_____ 125-mL flasks labeled "A," "B," and "C" (3)

Demonstration/Supplies Table

For each class

_____ compound microscopes labeled "A" and "B" (2)
_____ slide of living *Elodea* in DI water (1)
_____ slide of living *Elodea* in concentrated NaCl solution (1)
_____ toothpicks (to make the slides)
_____ petroleum jelly (to seal the slides)
_____ carrot or celery in beaker of DI water (1)
_____ carrot or celery in beaker of concentrated NaCl solution (1)
_____ demonstration experiment of ox blood in hypotonic, isotonic, and hypertonic solutions
1-L flasks, each labeled and filled with one of the following solutions:
_____ DI water (1)
_____ 0.1 *M* sucrose (1)
_____ 0.2 *M* sucrose (1)
_____ 0.3 *M* sucrose (1)
_____ 0.4 *M* sucrose (1)
_____ 0.5 *M* sucrose (1)
_____ 0.6 *M* sucrose (1)
_____ 150–250-mL beakers with approximate graduations labeled for each of the above solutions (7)
_____ balances (2)

Instructor's Desk

For each class

_____ projection technology (computer with digital projector or document camera, or overhead projector)
_____ Tables 3.5 and 3.6 downloaded in Excel format from www.masteringbiology.com
_____ USB drive
_____ transparencies of Table 3.4 and Table 3.5 (if computers are not available)
_____ washable pens (if computers are not available)
_____ photomicroscopy system (optional)

Grocery Supplies

For each four students

_____ baking potato (1)
_____ 9-oz plastic cups (7)

For each class

_____ sugar (1.5 lb)

Solutions/Chemicals

For each four students

small bottles or dropper bottles of:
_____ water (1)
_____ I_2KI (1)

_____ Benedict's solution (1)
_____ glucose test strips (optional)
_____ oxen blood (1)
small beakers of:
_____ 30% glucose (dextrose) (1)
_____ 1% starch (1)
125-mL flasks labeled:
_____ A (DI water) (1)
_____ B (0.154 M NaCl) (1)
_____ C (concentrated NaCl solution) (1)
_____ small container of carmine powder (1)

LAB TOPIC 4

Enzymes

First, decide how many student teams there will be in a given lab period. Each lab room should have at least one team performing each of the experiments in Exercise 4.3, the effects of concentration, pH, and temperature on amylase activity. In a lab of 24 students, we have six teams. Two teams perform the concentration experiment, two the pH experiment, and two the temperature experiment.

For this laboratory we dispense lab materials on cafeteria trays, one tray for each lab team (group of four students). We prepare each tray with the supplies in common for all experiments; then we label the trays for one of the experiments in Exercise 4.3 (the amylase experiments) to indicate if it is the pH, concentration, or temperature experiment. After that we add the supplies necessary for those particular experiments to the appropriate tray. The lab preparator should determine which student team will perform each experiment and place the appropriate tray in that team's work area. Supplies that are on demonstration tables can then be located near the appropriate team. For example, we place the water baths on a demonstration table near the team performing the temperature experiment.

Before and after lab, refrigerate all solutions and carry them to the laboratory just before lab begins. Note that many of the chemicals are toxic (catechol, PTU, and the buffers). Have a disposal plan in place before lab begins. Check with your school's safety officer.

In this edition of the laboratory manual we have added a new organizing table and instructions for preparing the serial dilutions of the amylase in Exercise 4.3, Experiment A. We hope this will help students understand the process as they carry out the precise steps required to dilute the amylase for this experiment.

Note: We use deionized water (DI water) in all our preps. Distilled water can be substituted, depending on availability.

Remember that 20 drops = 1 mL.

For Each Four Students

- computer with Tables 4.5, 4.6, and 4.7 downloaded in Excel format from www.masteringbiology.com. Students select Study Area, Lab Media, Investigating Biology Lab Data Tables — 9th edition. Instructors select Instructor Resources. In Instructor Home, select Instructor Guides for Supplements, and then Data Tables from Investigating Biology Lab Manual, 9e. Students can record their data and analyze the results.
- USB drive

The following items should be placed on a tray (one tray per four students):

- 1 test-tube rack
- 6 small test tubes (13 mm × 100 mm or to hold about 8 mL)
- 10 standard test tubes (16 mm × 150 mm or to hold about 20 mL)

- small Parafilm™ squares (Carolina Biological Supply # 215600)
- wax pencil
- 1 pipette pump
- 1 5-mL calibrated pipette* (Leave this in the flask of DI water.)
- 7 1-mL calibrated pipettes*
- 4 disposable Pasteur pipettes or transfer pipettes (Fisher, # 13-711-9A) (Optional— use in place of 1-mL calibrated pipettes. We usually put both 5.75- and 9-in. pipettes on each tray. You may choose to have additional pipettes available in the room.)
- 2 small pipette bulbs (the small balloon type for Pasteur pipettes)
- flask of DI water (250 mL)
- beaker of DI water to rinse pipettes
- dropper bottles of:
    DI water
    1% catechol
    1% phenylthiourea (PTU)
    potato extract (not potato starch)
    I_2KI solution
- 1–2 test plates**
- small trash disposal container

Exercise 4.3, Experiments A, B, C

Use the following table as a guide as you prepare trays for each experiment (amounts of solutions are more than enough for each application).

	A (conc.)	B (pH)	C (temp.)
5- or 10-mL graduated cylinder	1	—	—
1-mL calibrated pipette	1	—	1
5-mL calibrated pipette	2	2	1
small flask, buffer pH 6.8	15 mL	—	5 mL
flask of 1% starch	5 mL	20 mL	25 mL
flask of 1% amylase	10 mL	10 mL	10 mL

To the pH Trays (Experiment B), Add:

- small flasks of buffers: pH 4, 5, 6, 7, 8, 9

    The experiment calls for 5 mL of each of these. We add enough buffer to the flasks to last several days. At the end of each day we pour all the buffer of one pH together and check

---

*Pipettes may be labeled with tape and reused in subsequent labs.
**The test plates we prefer are white plastic, approximate dimensions 19 cm × 28 cm, with 96 depressions. In recent years we have had difficulty locating a supplier for the white plates, but clear plastic plates are available from Fisher Scientific, # 07-200-86 (48 wells) or # 07-200-87 (96 wells). We buy 48-well plates. If you use clear plates, have students place them over a piece of white paper to be able to see the I_2KI color change. We do not allow the students to write on the plates. It is impossible to remove marks. Have the students label rows by placing the plate over a piece of paper with the edge of the paper extending beyond the plate and writing the labels on the paper. Warn students to wash the plates carefully after they have finished the experiment. They are impossible to clean after they have dried soiled. We have tried to clean them with a bleach solution with limited success.

the pH and redispense it into the flasks. We usually have to discard the buffers and supply fresh solutions after about three labs. Buffers with the pH lying between these points may be used also, but we find this new distribution gives an adequate curve.

- pH paper

Demonstration/Supplies Table

Exercise 4.3, Experiment C

- 80°C water bath with test-tube rack and thermometer
- 37°C water bath with test-tube rack and thermometer
- test-tube rack at room temperature
- beaker of crushed ice with thermometer
- disposable gloves (optional)

Instructor's Desk

- projection technology (computer with digital projector or document camera, or overhead projector)
- USB drive
- Tables 4.5, 4.6, and 4.7 downloaded in Excel format from www.masteringbiology.com in Instructor Resources. Students can record their data and analyze the results.

Grocery Supplies

- potatoes (1 medium potato per two labs of 24 students each)

Solution Preparation Notes

Adjust amounts according to your needs.

1% Catechol

1. Add 1 g catechol (Carolina Biological Supply # 853540) to 100 mL DI water.
2. Stir until dissolved.
3. This makes enough solution for one lab of 24 students. Make fresh catechol each term. The solution is clear immediately after mixing and turns yellow as it stands. It turns light brown when mixed with potato extract.

 Catechol is a poison. Avoid contact with solutions. Wash hands thoroughly after preparing solutions. If a spill occurs, wear disposable gloves and use dry paper towels to wipe up the spill. Follow the dry towels with towels soaked in soap and water. Dispose of all towels in the trash.

1% Starch

1. Add 1 g potato starch (Sigma-Aldrich #'s S2004, S4251, Carolina Biological Supply # 892532) to 100 mL DI water.

2. Heat and stir with a magnetic stirrer until the solution just boils.
3. Immediately remove it from the heat to prevent scorching. The starch must go into solution. If the starch is in solution, it will change from opaque to slightly translucent—a "glowing" appearance.
4. If a precipitate is still present, return the solution to a boil.
5. This is just enough for two labs of 24 students each.

1% Phenylthiourea (PTU)

1. Add 1 g PTU (Carolina Biological Supply # 881222) to 100 mL DI water.
2. Stir with a magnetic stirrer for 10–15 minutes. Not all of the PTU will go into solution.
3. Make this solution fresh every second day.
4. The amount (100 mL) is enough for at least eight labs of 24 students each.

 PTU is a poison. Avoid contact with solutions. Wash hands thoroughly after preparing solutions. If a spill occurs, wear disposable gloves and use dry paper towels to wipe up the spill. Follow the dry towels with towels soaked in soap and water. Dispose of all towels in the trash.

Potato Extract

1. Cut one or two washed potatoes into small pieces, including the skin, and place them in a blender with about 300 mL of DI water.
2. Blend well.
3. Strain through cheesecloth and add the supernatant to the dropper bottles.
4. Potato extract must be made fresh daily. Make it just before lab and refrigerate it with the bottles tightly stoppered until the last minute.
5. The amount will be enough for four labs of 24 students each.

6.8 Buffers

Mix pH 6 and pH 7 buffers described on the next page to create pH 6.8 buffer.

1% Amylase

1. Prepare fresh amylase each lab day. Dissolve 1 g amylase in 100 mL DI water. Centrifuge the solution or filter through several layers of cheesecloth.
2. Pipette the supernatant into dropper bottles and refrigerate until dispensed on student trays.

We purchase amylase from Sigma-Aldrich, # A3176, which is actually pancreatic amylase (salivary amylase is much more expensive). The results of the experiment will not be affected. The optimum pH for salivary amylase is 6.7, and for pancreatic amylase, 6.7–7.0. We have the students make predictions about salivary amylase in the lab exercise because at this stage in the course students are more likely to know the pH of the mouth than that of the duodenum.

Buffers

For Exercise 4.2, Experiment B, you will need buffers with pH 4, 5, 6, 7, 8, and 9, and for Exercise 4.2, Experiments A and C, you will need pH 6.8. Purchase packages of pre-mixed buffer powders such as the following from Carolina Biological Supply:

pH 4	cat. # 849350
pH 5	cat. # 849360
pH 6	cat. # 849370
pH 7	cat. # 849380
pH 8	cat. # 849390
pH 9	cat. # 849400

Follow the directions on the package to prepare 500 mL of each. Using a pH meter, measure the pH and adjust the pH if needed using 1–2 drops of 0.1 N HCl or 1–2 drops of 5% NaOH. Note that you will use buffers with pH 3, 5, 7, 9, and 11 in Lab Topic 5 Cellular Respiration and Fermentation, so as you order buffers for Lab Topic 2, add other pHs and increase amounts to cover Lab Topic 5. Once prepared, buffer solutions have a shelf life of 3 weeks. Store them refrigerated in an airtight container. Carolina Biological Supply includes a buffer preservative with each carton of buffers that extends the refrigerated shelf life to 3 months.

> Avoid contact with all buffer solutions. Wash hands thoroughly after preparing solutions. If a spill occurs, wear disposable gloves and use dry paper towels to wipe up the spill. Follow the dry towels with towels soaked in soap and water. Dispose of all towels in the trash.

I_2KI Solution

1. To make 1000 mL, dissolve 20 g of potassium iodide (KI) (Carolina Biological Supply # 883789) in 1000 mL DI water. Dissolve 10 g of iodine (Carolina Biological Supply # 868982) in the KI solution.
2. Store this stock solution in a large dark bottle. I_2KI solutions break down in light. The day of lab, pour some of the stock into a beaker and dilute it with water before dispensing it into the students' dropper bottles. Dilute until the solution is just dark enough to give the positive purple test with starch. If the I_2KI is too dark, it will stain the test plates.

We dispense the I_2KI in clear dropper bottles and keep them in a dark cabinet until we place them on student trays. We use the clear bottles so we can quickly check the color on subsequent lab days. We collect all I_2KI droppers at the end of lab and put them in the dark until the following lab day. This means that the iodine is in the light for the entire lab period and will break down more quickly than it would in dark dropper bottles. However, we think it is worth the inconvenience to be able to visually check the concentration.

Checklist of Materials

Equipment

For each four students

_____ Tables 4.5, 4.6, and 4.7 downloaded in Excel format from www.mastering-biology.com
_____ USB drive

_____ test-tube rack (1)
_____ wax pencil (1)
_____ small pipette bulbs (small balloon-type bulbs for Pasteur pipettes) (2–4)
_____ pipette pump (1)
_____ Parafilm squares
_____ pH paper (Exercise 4.3, Experiment B only)

Glassware

For each four students

_____ small test tubes (13 mm × 100 mm or to hold about 8 mL) (6)
_____ standard test tubes (16 mm × 150 mm or to hold about 20 mL) (8)
_____ test plates (1–2)
_____ 5-mL calibrated pipette (1)
_____ 1-mL calibrated pipettes (7)
_____ disposable 5.75-in. Pasteur pipettes (2) (alternative for calibrated pipettes)
_____ disposable 9-in. Pasteur pipettes (2) (alternative for calibrated pipettes)
_____ 5–10-mL graduated cylinder: (1), Exercise 4.3, Experiment A
_____ 1-mL calibrated pipettes: (1), Experiment A; (1), Experiment C
_____ 5-mL calibrated pipettes: (2), Experiment A; (2), Experiment B; (1), Experiment C
_____ trash disposal container (1)

Demonstration/Supplies Table

For each class

_____ 80°C water bath with test-tube rack and thermometer (1)
_____ 37°C water bath with test-tube rack and thermometer (1)
_____ test-tube rack with thermometer (room temperature) (1)
_____ beaker of crushed ice with thermometer (0°C) (1)
_____ box of disposable gloves (1)

Instructor's Desk

For each class

_____ projection technology (computer with digital projector or document camera, or overhead projector)
_____ Tables 4.5, 4.6, and 4.7 downloaded in Excel format
_____ USB drive
_____ graph paper (optional)
_____ colored pencils (1 box of three colors) (optional)
_____ blank transparencies for teams to present results (if computers are not available)
_____ washable pens (6) (if computers are not available)

Grocery Supplies

_____ potatoes (1 per student team—usually four students)

Solutions/Chemicals

For each four students

_____ flask with 25 mL of DI water (1)
_____ flask with 1% amylase (1)
_____ beaker of DI water to rinse pipettes (1)
_____ flask of 1% starch (1)
dropper bottles of:
_____   1% catechol (1)
_____   DI water (1)
_____   potato extract (1)
_____   1% phenylthiourea (PTU) (1)
_____ I_2KI solution (1)
small flasks of buffers:
_____   pH 4 (1), Experiment B
_____   pH 5 (1), Experiment B
_____   pH 6 (1), Experiment B
_____   pH 6.8 (1), Experiments A and C
_____   pH 7 (1), Experiment B
_____   pH 8 (1), Experiment B
_____   pH 9 (1), Experiment B

Cellular Respiration and Fermentation

The organization for this lab topic is similar to that of several other lab topics in this laboratory program (for example, Lab Topics 21 and 26), where students first perform experiments using procedures given in the lab manual (called Experiment A), and then perform another experiment using their own design. Exercise 5.1, Experiment A, investigates fermentation, and Exercise 5.2, Experiment A, investigates cellular respiration. In Exercise 5.3, students design and perform an additional experiment with either fermentation or cellular respiration. Experiment B in each exercise gives students suggestions for their original experiment. New in this edition, we have included a template that can be used to assist student teams in developing their proposals. Using a template will simplify evaluating their proposals and preparing the materials needed for their open-inquiry investigations.

The person preparing supplies for this lab topic should prepare all supplies for Experiment A in Exercises 5.1 and 5.2. However, there is some flexibility for Exercise 5.3. Place all supplies for each Experiment A on trays, one for each student research team. Have supplies for the students' original experiments on a supply table. You may limit or expand the supplies available for this exercise depending on your particular situation. Have a PowerPoint slide or overhead transparency in each lab room listing available supplies for Exercise 5.3. If possible, be ready to prepare or locate additional materials if students have requests. If possible, instruct students to turn in a supply list several days before the lab so you will have their specific materials available.

You may have one of three different models of spectrophotometers in your laboratory. The analog Spectronic 20 is a reliable model used in introductory biology labs for years. The digital Thermo Scientific Spectronic 20D+ is a more recent model, and the latest model offered by Thermo Scientific is the digital Spectronic 200. This latest model replaces the Spectronic 20 and 20D+ models. Instructions for operating the digital Thermo Scientific Spectronic 20D+ are given in the laboratory manual in Lab Topics 5 and 6 and in Appendix C, Techniques and Instrumentation, in the laboratory manual. Instructions for operating the Spectronic 200 are also included in that appendix. Instructions for operating the Spectronic 20 are included in this chapter of the Preparation Guide. Post instructions for operating the particular spectrophotometers that you use in your laboratories near each instrument.

For Each Four Students

- computer with Tables 5.2 and 5.4 downloaded in Excel format from www.masteringbiology.com. Students should select Study Area, Lab Media, Investigating Biology Lab Data Tables — 9th edition. Instructors go to Instructor Resources, Instructor Guides for Supplements, and then Data Tables from Investigating Biology Lab Manual, 9e. Students can record their data and analyze the results. These tables can also be modified by students for their independent investigation.
- USB drive

Exercise 5.1, Experiment A

- water bath set at 30°C (Two student groups may share one bath.)
- 4 respirometers, each consisting of the following:
    1 125-mL flask
    1 standard test tube
    1 1-mL graduated pipette with a 16-cm-long piece of aquarium tubing attached
    1 medium binder clip
    1 metal weight. Purchase 3–4 in. doughnut-shaped metal weights at a hardware store. These weights should be able to fit over the neck of the flask to keep the flask from tipping over in the water bath. We use "standard steel zinc plated" washers purchased from MSC Industrial Supply Company, # 67489328, 3½″ diameter.
- pipette pump to fit aquarium tubing
- pipette pump to fit 5-mL graduated pipettes
- about 20 mL of 10% glucose solution in a small beaker
- about 20 mL of freshly made yeast solution in a small beaker
- a flask of DI water
- three 5-mL pipettes: label one "H_2O," the second "yeast," and the third "glucose"
- 400–600-mL beaker with DI water. (Keep the various pipettes in this and use as rinse water.)
- wax marking pencil

Exercise 5.2, Experiment A

- 4 identical cuvettes or small test tubes that fit the spectrophotometer
- 150-mL beaker to hold the cuvettes
- spectrophotometer (Two student groups may share, but the lab goes more smoothly if you have one per group.)
- Kimwipes beside each spectrophotometer
- graduated pipettes, one of each labeled:
    mitochondria (a 1-mL pipette)
    DPIP (a 1-mL pipette)
    succinate (a 1-mL pipette)
    buffer (a 5-mL pipette)
- Keep the following on ice until students are ready to perform this experiment. Have one for each group of students, and cover each with a small square of Parafilm:
    5 mL of DPIP in a 10-mL test tube (Wrap tubes with foil.)
    5 mL 0.025 M succinate in a 10-mL test tube
    5 mL mitochondria suspension in a 10-mL test tube
    about 25 mL of phosphate buffer, pH 7.2, in a 50-mL beaker
- 4 small squares of Parafilm to cover the experimental tubes
- wax pencil
- pipette pump
- test-tube rack

Exercise 5.3

- All supplies available for the Experiment A part of Exercises 5.1 and 5.2 are available for this exercise. However, additional amounts of yeast suspension and phosphate buffer may be needed. Have additional beakers, flasks, pipettes, and graduated cylinders available. Have disposable gloves for those students working with toxic chemicals.

For Exercise 5.1, Experiment B, have about 100 mL of the following solutions available for students who choose to work with fermentation. Place a labeled beaker beside each labeled container to dispense the solution and prevent contamination. Once the solutions are prepared, they can be used all week.

- 10% sucrose
- 10% honey
- 10% molasses
- 10% corn syrup
- 10% agave nectar
- 10% glycogen
- packets of sugar substitutes
- different strains of yeasts (do not use brewer's yeast from a health food store)
- series of buffers: pH 3, 5, 7, 9, 11
- sodium fluoride solutions: 0.01, 0.03, 0.06 M
- sodium benzoate (inhibits at 0.5% solution)
- 30% ethyl alcohol
- 10% pyruvate
- $MgSO_4$
- 5% NaCl
- powdered spices in solution (see Grocery Supplies)

If students choose to make their own solutions of spices, have a mortar and pestle and balance available to grind and weigh the spices. Remind them to clean the mortar and pestle after use.

For Exercise 5.2, Experiment B, have these additional solutions available with a labeled beaker to dispense the solutions:

- 10% fructose
- 10% glucose
- 10% maltose
- 1% starch (Higher concentrations will be too thick.)
- Rotenone
- oligomycin
- antimycin A
- $CuSO_4$
- berberine
- curcumin
- quercetin

Demonstration/Supplies Table

- If you do not have water baths and spectrophotometers at each student desk, have these on the demonstration table, if possible, one for each group of four students. Post operating instructions beside each spectrophotometer. Instructions for operating the digital Thermo Scientific Spectronic 20D+ are given in the laboratory manual in Lab Topics 5 and 6 and also in Appendix C in the laboratory manual. Instructions for operating the Spectronic 200 are also included in Appendix C. Instructions for the Spectronic 20 are found on the next page.
- box of Kimwipes, 1 per spectrophotometer
- ice box with ice and a test-tube rack (In this rack place tubes of DPIP, mitochondria suspension, and succinate. Also have flasks of phosphate buffer on ice.)
- mortar and pestle
- balance

Operating Instructions for the Spectronic 20

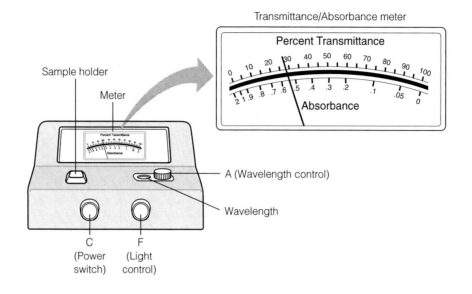

1. Connect the Spectronic 20 to an electrical outlet. Turn on the power (C–power switch). Allow 15 minutes warmup time.
2. Select the beginning wavelength. Turn the wavelength control knob (A) to the proper setting. For the photosynthesis experiment, begin at 400. For the cellular respiration experiment, the wavelength remains at 600 throughout.
3. With no sample tube in place and the sample holder cover closed, turn the zero control knob (same as the power switch C) and bring the meter needle to 0% transmittance.
4. Insert the blank (cuvette A—reference material only) into the sample holder and close the lid. Adjust the light control (F) until the meter reads 100% transmittance (0 absorbance).
5. Remove the blank and insert the test cuvette (with pigment). Record the absorbance reading from the meter. (Record % transmittance in Lab Topic 5.)
6. Select a new wavelength. (Wavelength remains at 600 nm in Lab Topic 5.)
7. Repeat steps 4–6 until all readings have been taken, bringing the meter to 100% transmittance with the blank before each new absorbance reading.

Instructor's Desk

- projection technology (computer with digital projector or document camera, or overhead projector)
- Tables 5.2 and 5.4 downloaded in Excel format from www.masteringbiology.com in Instructor Resources.
- USB drive
- PowerPoint or overhead transparency with list of supplies available for independent investigations

Grocery Supplies

- yeast (We purchase 4-oz jars of Fleischmann's Bread Machine yeast, available at most grocery stores. You may use packages of yeast. If you purchase rapid-rise yeast, adjust yeast concentrations.)

- lima beans (Purchase dried lima beans from Carolina Biological, # 158335. We have found these work better than those purchased from the grocery store.)
- various substrates: honey, molasses, sugar substitutes (saccharin, Splenda, Stevia), corn syrup, agave nectar
- various types of yeasts (Check health food stores, home brewing supply stores, local bakers, and the Web): dry active, quick rise, Pasteur champagne, sourdough (*Candida milleri*), beer brewing yeast (*S. cerevisiae* and *S. pastorianus*)
- various spices: ground cinnamon, cloves, carraway, ginger, cardamom, nutmeg, mace, thyme, mustard, hot peppers, cayenne pepper, celery seed, turmeric, oregano, sage, fennel, cloves
- peaches, cassava root

Solution Preparation Notes

Yeast Suspension

Make about 50 mL of yeast suspension for each lab section of 24 students. Make a fresh yeast suspension for each lab day. Leftover yeast may be used by a subsequent lab period in the same day.

Use 7 grams of yeast per 50 mL of tap water. (Use half this amount if using rapid-rise yeast.) The water should be about 37–45°C. Run tap water until it feels warm but not so hot that it will kill the yeast. If you are unsure, use a thermometer. If you add a drop of red food coloring to the yeast suspension, students may be able to read the graduated pipette more easily.

"Rapid-rise" yeast is advertised as being 50% faster than typical yeast, so if you use this type of yeast for Exercise 5.1, Experiment A, adjust concentrations accordingly.

Mitochondria Suspension

 Lima beans must be soaked overnight before they are used to prepare mitochondria!

Weigh 50 g of dried lima beans in a 250-mL beaker. Cover with excess water and place in the refrigerator overnight. Put the clean (chemical-free) blender cup, a 1000-mL beaker, and all containers that will hold the mitochondria in the freezer (for example, centrifuge tubes, a beaker to collect the supernatant, and the small test tubes used to dispense the mitochondrial suspension to each student group). All solutions should be in the refrigerator.

For best results, we recommend that you begin preparing the mitochondria suspension about 1 hour before the lab begins, although we have had good results with mitochondria refrigerated overnight.
1. Pour off the liquid, and place the beans in the blender cup with 100-mL sucrose-phosphate buffer (not phosphate buffer). Blend at high speed for 2 minutes.
2. Set the cold 1000-mL beaker in an ice bucket with ice. Strain the bean homogenate through cheesecloth into this beaker. Squeeze the cheesecloth gently to get the filtrate through.
3. Divide the filtrate equally among several centrifuge tubes.
4. Centrifuge at 200 × g (or a low setting) for 1 minute (to separate the largest cellular particles). Increase the speed and centrifuge at 1300 × g (or a medium-high setting) for 10 minutes. This settles larger cellular particles, but the mitochondria will stay in the supernatant.

5. Decant the supernatant from each centrifuge tube into a beaker, and then pour it from the beaker into small test tubes, one for each student research team. Place these small test tubes on ice in a test-tube rack in an ice chest, one ice chest per lab room.

DPIP (0.5%)

After the DPIP is added to the mitochondrial solution, transmission must be between 5% and 30%. *The mitochondria experiment will fail if the DPIP is not the correct concentration,* and, unfortunately, if different sources or ages of the powdered DPIP are used, the recipe does not make consistent solutions. We have found that we must check the DPIP solution every semester to be sure that it is the correct concentration for spectrophotometry. If you used previous editions of this preparation guide, you will note that the following recipe is more dilute than in previous editions.

Make the DPIP fresh daily. To make 100 mL, dissolve 0.5 g DPIP powder (2,6 dichloro-indophenol sodium salt, available from Sigma-Aldrich, # D 1878) in 100 mL DI water (0.5% solution). Mix the powder and water in a dark bottle or use a flask covered with foil. Stir on a stirring plate for about 30 minutes, until completely dissolved. This will be your stock solution. *Dilute this stock solution 1 part to 15 parts DI water* (10 mL stock solution in 150 mL DI water). 100 mL is enough for a lab of 24 students. Dispense about 5–10 mL of the diluted solution in small test tubes covered with foil, one for each student research team. Place these tubes on ice in the test-tube rack with the mitochondrial suspension.

We *strongly* recommend that you check the concentration of DPIP before lab after you have made up the mitochondrial solution. To do this, mix 4.4 mL buffer and 0.3 mL mitochondrial solution in a cuvette and use this solution to bring the spectrophotometer to 100% transmittance. Then add 0.3 mL DPIP and measure transmittance of this solution. The initial reading should be between about 5% and 30% transmittance. *If it is more than 30% transmittance,* your solution is too dilute. Make up a new, more concentrated DPIP dilution using the initial 0.5% stock solution. If *transmittance is less than 5%* the DPIP solution is too concentrated. In this case, add more water to the 1:15 DPIP. An alternate plan is to have the students work with the DPIP until they get an appropriate dilution. When they set up the experiment, have them use the diluted stock. If transmittance is greater than 30%, they can add an additional 0.3 mL DPIP to each tube, or they can dilute the DPIP if transmission is less than 5%.

Succinate (0.025 *M*)

To make 1000 mL, dissolve 2.95 g succinic acid (Fisher # BP336-500 or Sigma-Aldrich # S 7501) in 1000 mL DI water. Dispense about 10–15 mL of the solution in small test tubes, one for each student research team. Place these tubes on ice in the test-tube rack with the mitochondria and DPIP.

Phosphate Buffer

To make 1 liter of 7.2 phosphate buffer, first prepare the following two solutions:

Solution A (0.2 *M* KH_2PO_4) (monobasic potassium phosphate)

Dissolve 27.22 g KH_2PO_4 (Fisher Scientific # BP362-500, Sigma-Aldrich # P 5379) in 600 mL DI water. Bring volume up to 1000 mL with DI water.

Solution B (0.2 M K$_2$HPO$_4$) (dibasic potassium phosphate)

Dissolve 34.84 g K$_2$HPO$_4$ (Fisher Scientific # BP363-500, Sigma-Aldrich # P 3786) in 600 mL DI water. Bring volume up to 1000 mL with DI water.

For 1 liter of buffer, mix 280 mL Solution A with 720 mL Solution B. The pH should be 7.2. Adjust by adding Solution A if pH is too high, or Solution B if pH is too low.

Sucrose Phosphate Buffer

The sucrose phosphate buffer is used to make the mitochondrial suspension only, and is prepared using the phosphate buffer above. You will need approximately 20 mL of sucrose phosphate buffer per group of four students.

To make 1 liter:

Dissolve 136.9 g sucrose in phosphate buffer, pH 7.2 (previous recipe). The pH should be 7.2. Adjust as described for the phosphate buffer if necessary and bring to 1 liter.

Solutions for Exercise 5.3, Student-Designed Investigations

Make up the substrates as 10% stock solutions. Students can then dilute the stock to fit their respective experiments.

For 10% solutions of **sucrose** (Sigma-Aldrich # S 7903), **glucose** (Sigma-Aldrich # G 8270), **fructose** (Sigma-Aldrich # F 0127, Fisher # L96-500), and **maltose** (Sigma-Aldrich # M 2250), dissolve 10 g of the powder in 100 mL DI water. **Glycogen** extracted from several different animal sources is available from suppliers. We suggest Sigma-Aldrich # G 8751 from oysters and G 0885 from bovine liver (less expensive). To make a 10% solution, dissolve 10 g in 100 mL DI water.

1% Starch (Sigma-Aldrich # S 4251—potato starch, Carolina Biological Supply # 892532):

Dissolve 1 g per 100 mL DI water. Heat until completely dissolved and solution begins to appear translucent.

For 10% solutions of **liquid substrates,** mix 10 mL with 90 mL DI water. Do not measure the liquid substrates with a graduated cylinder. These syrups are very difficult to remove. Measure in a graduated beaker.

For **sugar substitute** solutions, make 1% solutions or very small amounts of 10% solutions.

For **spice solutions,** be sure spices are in ground form. Have a mortar and pestle available. Dry spices are difficult to get into solution. First, make a paste of the spices with a small amount of water. Then, dilute with the remaining water and mix well. Use solutions at concentrations no more than 5–10% of the weight of yeast used in the experiment. For example, if students are using a 1% yeast solution in their experiment, then the spice used in the experiment should be a 0.1% solution. Students might make up a 1% solution and then dilute this to test various concentrations.

Salt solutions: Have students begin with a 5% solution (5 grams in 100 mL DI water) and then dilute this.

Yeast solutions: If comparing different types of yeast, make all the same concentration (see page 31).

Plant extracts: Prepare a crude extract of soft plant material by weighing out 2 g of the material: fruits (peppers), leaves (sweet clover), roots (cassava), or seeds (foxglove).

Pulverize in a mortar and pestle, adding a small amount of water until you have added 100 mL total. Stir the solution for 15 minutes. Filter through cheesecloth or filter paper. This will be a stock solution that can then be diluted by 50% or more. For peach pits, first remove and discard the flesh, then carefully break the hard pit with a hammer. Remove the inner soft seed and proceed as above.

Prepare a crude extract of woody material: cinnamon sticks, black walnut bark or husks, or red oak bark. Cut or shave the bark or sticks into small pieces. Weigh out 2 g of material and add to 100 mL of water. Heat to 60°C with continuous stirring for 20 minutes. Alternatively, the material can stir unheated overnight. Filter through cheesecloth or filter paper and cool. This will be a stock solution that can be diluted by 50% or more.

Additional Solutions for Exercise 5.3

MgSO$_4$ (Sigma-Aldrich # M 7506): make a 1% stock solution. Add 1 g MgSO$_4$ to 100 mL DI H$_2$O. Students may dilute the solution.

0.05 *M* Malonate (Sigma-Aldrich # M 1875): dissolve 0.74 g in 100 mL phosphate buffer, pH 7.2

CuSO$_4$: 25 mg per 100 mL DI water

Buffer Series: pH 3, 5, 7, 9, 11

We purchase respective buffers in Chemvelope from Carolina Biological Supply. Dissolve the contents of these packages in 500 mL DI water to produce the appropriate pH. For pH 3, Carolina Biological Supply # 849340; pH 5, # 849360; pH 7, # 849380; pH 9, # 849400; pH 11, # 849420.

> Check with your school safety officer before using the following chemicals! Powders of these substances are toxic. Only the professional prep person should prepare the solutions. Prepare in a hood. Do not breathe the chemical dust. Wear protective gloves and eyewear. Do not allow students to make up these solutions! Do not take chemicals in powder form into the students' laboratory! Supply gloves and eye protection for students as they work with the solutions.

Antimycin A (Sigma-Aldrich # A 8674):

To make a stock solution, dissolve 1 mg/mL in 100% ethanol. This is stable as a stock solution at 4°C for several months. Dilute this stock solution 100 times in DI water for student experiments. Students may again dilute this 10–100 times for their experiments. Antimycin A is a fungicidal antibiotic. It inhibits the reduction of cytochrome *b*.

Rotenone (Sigma-Aldrich # R 8875):

To make a stock solution, dissolve 1 mg/mL in 100% dimethyl sulfoxide (DMSO) (Sigma # D 5879). Refrigerate at 4°C. Dilute this stock solution 100 times in DI water for student experiments. Students may again dilute this 10–100 times for their experiments. Check also with your local feed and seed supply. This is sold in 1% powders to be used as a pesticide in gardens. Concentrations higher than this are used to kill fish in ponds.

Oligomycin (Sigma-Aldrich # O 4876):

To make a stock solution, dissolve 1 mg/mL in 100% DMSO. Refrigerate at 4°C. Dilute this stock solution 100 times in DI water for student experiments. Students may again dilute this 10–100 times for their experiments.

Sodium Fluoride (Sigma-Aldrich # S 1504):

Make up a 0.1 M solution in DI water. Students may dilute this for their experiments. To make 0.1 M, dissolve 4.2 g in 1000 mL DI water.

Curcumin (VWR #B21573-09)

To make a 1% stock solution, dissolve 1g in 1 mL of 100% ethanol then add 99 mL of DI water. Refrigerate at 4°C. Students may again dilute this 10–100 times for their experiments.

Berberine (VWR #L03807-06)

To make a 1% stock solution, dissolve 1g in 1 mL of 100% ethanol then add 99 mL of DI water. Refrigerate at 4°C. Students may again dilute this 10–100 times for their experiments.

Quercetin (VWR #AC17407-0100)

To make a 1% stock solution, dissolve 1g in 1 mL of 100% DMSO then add 99 mL of DI water. Refrigerate at 4°C. Students may again dilute this 10–100 times or more for their experiments.

Checklist of Materials

Equipment

For each four students

_____ computer with Tables 5.2 and 5.4 downloaded in Excel format from www.masteringbiology.com.
_____ USB drive
_____ 125-mL flasks (4)
_____ standard test tubes (4)
_____ 1-mL graduated pipettes with aquarium tubing attached (4)
_____ medium binder clip (4)
_____ pipette pump for aquarium tubing (1)
_____ doughnut-shaped metal ring (4)
_____ pipette pump for 5-mL graduated pipettes (1)
_____ 400–600-mL beaker with DI water
_____ 5-mL pipettes (4) labeled "H$_2$O," "yeast," "glucose," "buffer"
_____ 1-mL pipettes (3) labeled "mitochondria," "DPIP," "succinate"
_____ flask containing DI water (1)
_____ wax marking pencil (1)
_____ spectrophotometer
_____ box of Kimwipes
_____ cuvettes or small test tubes for spectrophotometer (4)
_____ 150-mL beaker (1)
_____ small squares of Parafilm

Solutions

_____ 10% glucose (20 mL)
_____ yeast (20 mL)
_____ phosphate buffer (on ice)
_____ DPIP (on ice)
_____ succinate (on ice)
_____ mitochondria suspension (on ice)

Demonstration/Supplies Table

_____ additional beakers
_____ additional flasks
_____ additional graduated and Pasteur pipettes
_____ mortar and pestle
_____ disposable gloves
_____ eye protection
_____ solutions: sucrose, honey, corn syrup, salt, glycogen, yeast varieties, various spices, series of buffers, sodium fluoride, ethyl alcohol, pyruvate, $MgSO_4$, fructose, glucose, maltose, starch, rotenone, oligomycin, antimycin A, $CuSO_4$, malonate, berberine, curcumin, quercetin

For each class

_____ water bath at 30°C (1 per student group)
_____ ice chest with ice and test-tube holder

Instructor's Desk

For each class

_____ projection technology (computer with digital projector or document camera, or overhead projector)
_____ Tables 5.2 and 5.4 downloaded in Excel format from www.masteringbiology.com
_____ PowerPoint or overhead transparency with list of supplies available for independent investigations
_____ USB drive

Grocery Supplies

_____ yeast (various types)
_____ fruits (peppers)
_____ baby lima beans, dried
_____ honey, molasses, sugar substitutes, corn syrup, agave nectar
_____ spices: cinnamon, cloves, carraway, ginger, cardamom, nutmeg, mace, thyme, mustard, hot peppers, cayenne pepper, turmeric, oregano, sage
_____ peaches (for pits), cassava root
_____ cassia cinnamon sticks

Field Collections

_____ red oak bark
_____ black walnut bark or husks

_____ sweet clover (leaves and stems)
_____ foxglove seeds

Mitochondrial Preparation Supplies

_____ blender (Keep cup in freezer.)
_____ centrifuge and centrifuge tubes (Keep tubes in freezer.)
_____ cheesecloth
_____ sucrose-phosphate buffer (in refrigerator)
_____ ice bucket
_____ 1000-mL beaker (in freezer)
_____ small test tubes to dispense mitochondria

Fermentation Research Proposal

Team Name: **Team Members:**

Date: **Instructor:**

Question:

Hypothesis:

Prediction:

Summary of the Procedures: Modify the table below (a variation of *Table 5.1*) to match your experimental procedures. Keep in mind that the total volume should be the same as the procedure in Experiment A. You may have up to 8 tubes in your research protocol. The last column is for your additional inhibitor or promoter if you are using one.

Tube	DI Water	Yeast Suspension	Substrate	

Materials: Think about additional materials or supplies that you will need for your experiment. List those here. If you are making a plant extract you will need a mortar and pestle and a balance to weigh the plant material. If you are using other substrates, reagents, or spices we will prepare a stock solution for you. *You can dilute the stock solutions by adding different volumes to your tubes.*

Respiration Research Proposal

Team Name: **Team Members:**

Date: **Instructor:**

Question:

Hypothesis:

Prediction:

Summary of the Procedures: Modify the table below (a variation of *Table 5.3*) to match your experimental procedures. Keep in mind that the total volume should be the same as the procedure in Experiment A. You may have up to 8 tubes in your research protocol. The last column is for your inhibitor or promoter if you are using one.

Tube	Phosphate Buffer	DPIP	Mitochondrial Suspension	Substrate	

Materials: Think about additional materials or supplies that you will need for your experiment. List those here. If you are making a plant extract you will need a mortar and pestle and a balance to weigh the plant material. If you are using other substrates, reagents, or spices we will prepare a stock solution for you. *You can dilute the stock solutions by adding different volumes to your tubes.*

LAB TOPIC 6

Photosynthesis

In this laboratory students perform several activities simultaneously and are organized into groups of different sizes. We group materials for each exercise (some on trays) and label them accordingly. Three to 4 weeks before the photosynthesis lab, determine the number of geranium and *Coleus* leaves needed for all laboratory sections and check greenhouse supplies. If you decide to grow lima beans, these must be started 3–4 weeks in advance to ensure enough leaves for the experiments.

You may have one of three different models of spectrophotometers in your laboratory. The analog Spectronic 20 is a reliable model used in introductory biology labs for years. The digital Thermo Scientific Spectronic 20D+ is a more recent model, and the latest model offered by Thermo Scientific is the digital Spectronic 200. This latest model replaces the Spectronic 20 and 20D+ models. Instructions for operating the digital Thermo Scientific Spectronic 20D+ are given in the laboratory manual Lab Topics 5 and 6 and in Appendix C, Techniques and Instrumentation, in the laboratory manual. Instructions for operating the Spectronic 200 are also included in that appendix. Instructions for operating the Spectronic 20 are included in Lab Topic 5 of this Preparation Guide. Post instructions for operating the particular spectrophotometers that you use in your laboratories near each instrument.

For Each Two Students

- 8–10-in. forceps for adding and removing leaves
- scissors

Exercise 6.2

- 1 multicolored *Coleus* leaf (A mix of green, white, purple, and pink is preferred.)
- dropper bottle of concentrated I_2KI

Exercise 6.3

- cylinder of chromatography paper (Carolina Biological Supply # 689110): 11 cm square, with light pencil line drawn 1.5–2 cm from bottom of the paper and then stapled into a cylinder
- capillary tube (0.4 mm ID, length 75 mm) to add the pigment to the pencil line (A fine brush may also work.)
- small test tube, beaker, or flask with chlorophyll extract, covered tightly with Parafilm (Carolina Biological Supply # 215600)
- quart jar with screw-top lid and chromatography solvent (Quart jars used for canning and available in grocery stores work well for this experiment.)

We keep these materials in the hood and have the students take their loaded chromatography paper cylinder to the hood to place it in the jar. If you keep the jars at the students' work area, warn students to keep them tightly closed and open them only briefly when adding the chromatography paper.

For Each Four Students

Exercises 6.1 and 6.2

- hot plate
- beaker tongs or heat-resistant gloves
- 1000-mL beaker with 300 mL of water
- 400-mL beaker with 200 mL of 80% ethyl alcohol
- 2 petri dishes with lids (100 mm × 20 mm)
- wash bottle with DI water

Exercise 6.4

- computers with Table 6.3 downloaded in Excel format from www.masteringbiology.com. Select Instructor Resources, Instructor Guides for Supplements, and then Data Tables from Investigating Biology Lab Manual, 9e. Students can record their data and analyze the results.
- 2 identical cuvettes
- 150-mL beaker to hold the 2 cuvettes
- 20–50-mL beaker for extracting pigment from chromatography paper
- 2 small corks to put in the cuvettes to prevent evaporation until absorption is measured

For Each Eight Students

Exercise 6.1

- 4 geranium leaves covered with a patch of either black construction paper or blue, green, or red plastic filters

  If students are adding the patches to the geranium leaves, have the following materials available during the lab prior to the photosynthesis lab; otherwise, the instructors will use the following to add patches to the leaves. (See Greenhouse Supplies section.)
- green, red, and blue plastic filters

  The plastic filters used in this exercise are designed to reflect and transmit the appropriate wavelengths of light to correspond to the visible spectrum. The filters absorb all other colors. For example, the green plastic filter transmits green light to the leaf, and the wavelengths of light that would be most efficient in photosynthesis are absorbed by this filter. Do not use cellophane available from local sources that might be designed for decorative uses. Red, blue, and green filters may be purchased from Barn Door Lighting Outfitters. We recommend that you purchase Rosco filters from this vendor. To transmit blue wavelengths, we recommend Rosco Cinegel R362S (transmits 32% at 480 nm). For green, choose Rosco Cinegel R386S (32% transmittance at 530 nm). For red, choose Rosco Cinegel R324S (31% transmittance at 660–700 nm). Collect plastic filters after each lab since they can be reused indefinitely.
- black heavyweight construction paper
- paper clips
- scissors

Demonstration/Supplies Table

- spectrophotometers (Preferred number is one per team of four students, but you can manage with fewer if teams share.) (See Teaching Plan.)
- box of Kimwipes, 1 per spectrophotometer
- extra chlorophyll extract, covered in a small beaker or flask
- *Coleus* plant with multicolored leaves (See Figure 6.3 in the laboratory manual.)

    Hand out individual leaves to each student team or have each team select one from the class plant.

Note: Instructions for operating the digital Spectronic 20D+ (now manufactured by Thermo Scientific) are given in Lab Topics 5 and 6 and in Appendix C of the laboratory manual. Procedures for operating the Spectronic 200 are also included in Appendix C. Instructions for the analog Spectronic 20 are provided in Lab Topic 5, Cellular Respiration and Fermentation, of this Preparation Guide. We recommend that you enlarge and photocopy instructions for the spectrophotometers that you are using and place a copy beside each instrument.

Supplies in the Hood

- acetone
- 3–5 10-mL graduated cylinders
- waste containers for discarded acetone and chlorophyll extract solutions

Instructor's Desk

- projection technology (computer with digital projector or document camera, or overhead projector)
- USB drive
- Table 6.3 downloaded in Excel format from www.masteringbiology.com in Instructor Resources. Students can record their data and analyze the results.

Greenhouse Supplies

- *Coleus* plant with multicolored leaves (at least one leaf per two students)

    The best source of multicolored *Coleus* plants is your local nursery. Those ordered from Carolina Biological Supply (#157312) may not have the three to four distinct colors that you need for the experiment (see Figure 6.3 in the laboratory manual).

    Keep plants well watered and in continuous bright lights for several days before the lab.

- geranium (*Pelargonium* sp.) plants (at least one leaf per two students)

    The instructor may have the students prepare these plants at the end of the previous week's lab. If the instructor chooses, these plants can be set up 4–5 days before the lab. *Once the treatment is applied, keep the plants on a 24-hr. bright light cycle.* Each group of eight students should have one leaf of each treatment: red, blue, and green plastic filters and black construction paper. Cut a rectangle of paper or plastic filter approximately 2.5 cm × 5 cm. Double over the strip and slide the edge of a healthy geranium leaf, still attached to the plant, between the folded edges. Carefully slip a slightly sprung paper clip over the paper, securing the paper to the leaf. The paper should cover both sides of the leaf. Return the plant to continuous bright light until the day of the lab. Plastic filters must transmit specific wavelengths of light. Do not use cellophane designed for decorative uses. You may use pieces of colorless transparency sheets held on with a paper clip as a second control.

- lima bean plants, if geranium plants are not available

  Begin germinating the seeds (Carolina Biological Supply # 158335) 3–4 weeks before the plants are needed. Apply all four treatments to one plant 5–7 days before the lab period. Provide one plant with at least four leaves per eight students.

- bean plants, if used for chlorophyll extract

  These should be started 3–4 weeks in advance as well.

Grocery Supplies

If spinach is used for chlorophyll extract, buy this fresh every 2 days. Be sure it is completely dry before extracting the pigments. We do not recommend using frozen spinach. Fresh grass clippings, fresh kale or turnip greens, bean plants grown in the greenhouse, or any other very green leafy vegetable can be used as an alternative to spinach.

Solution Preparation Notes

Chlorophyll Extract

If you are using a blender, chlorophyll extract can be made the day of the lab. Be very careful if you use a blender. It is possible to start a fire from a spark from the blender if the acetone spills. Cut up enough grass, turnip greens, fresh spinach, bean leaves, and so on, to fill the blender jar and add 200 mL of acetone. Cover and very carefully turn the blender on and off until all greens are chopped. Pour into a beaker and cover until just before the lab. Pour the chopped greens and acetone through cheesecloth to separate the extract. If you refrigerate the extract, it can be used for 2–3 days. Check early in the day to see if the extract is good, so more may be prepared if it is no longer usable. After 2 days, however, you may see additional bands (breakdown products).

If you do not have a blender, prepare the extract the day before. Use scissors to cut the greenery into very fine pieces. Soak the cut greenery in the acetone at room temperature tightly covered overnight. Pour through cheesecloth before using. The extract should appear dark green. One bunch of spinach makes 200 mL, more than enough extract for four labs of 24 students.

> Acetone is flammable. It is harmful if swallowed or inhaled. Use a hood to make solutions. Wash skin with soap and water if contact is made. If a spill occurs, eliminate all sources of ignition. Cover the spill with vermiculite or other absorbent material.

Chromatography Solvent

Use 9 parts petroleum ether (Carolina Biological Supply # 879542) and 1 part acetone (Carolina Biological Supply # 841502). Each quart jar will have approximately 1 cm of solvent (approximately 20 mL). Depending on the shape of the jars, the volume may vary.

> Petroleum ether is extremely flammable. It is harmful if swallowed or inhaled. Use a hood to make solutions. Avoid contact. Wash thoroughly after handling. If a spill occurs, eliminate all sources of ignition. Evacuate the area. Cover with an activated carbon absorbent, take up, and place in a closed container. Ventilate the area and wash the spill site. Wear heavy rubber gloves and use a self-contained breathing apparatus. If cleanup is not possible, evacuate the area. Keep all jars with the chromatography solvent in the hood as students use them.

I_2KI Iodine Potassium Iodide, Concentrated

To make 1000 mL:
1. Dissolve 20 g KI (potassium iodide—Carolina Biological Supply # 883789) in 1000 mL DI water. Dissolve 10 g iodine (Carolina Biological Supply # 868982) in the KI solution.
2. Store this stock solution in a large dark bottle. I_2KI solutions break down in light.

Dispense the I_2KI into clear dropper bottles and keep them in a dark cabinet until lab. We use the clear bottles so we can quickly check the color on subsequent lab days. We collect the bottles at the end of lab and put them in the dark until the following day. Alternatively, dispense solution in amber bottles.

Checklist of Materials

Equipment

For each two students

_____ cylinder of chromatography paper (1)
_____ forceps (1)
_____ scissors (1)

For each four students

_____ computer with Table 6.3 downloaded in Excel format from www.masteringbiology.com
_____ USB drive
_____ 8–10-in. forceps (1)
_____ hot plate (1)
_____ beaker tongs (or heat-resistant gloves) (1)

For each eight students

_____ green, red, and blue plastic filters (1 of each)
_____ black construction paper (1 sheet)
_____ paper clips (4)

Glassware

For each two students

_____ capillary tube (1)

For each four students

_____ 1000-mL beaker (for water) (1)
_____ 400-mL beaker (for alcohol) (1)
_____ petri dish with lid (1)
_____ cuvettes with cork stoppers (2)
_____ 150-mL beaker (for cuvettes) (1)
_____ 20–50-mL beaker (for diluting pigments) (1)

Demonstration/Supplies Table

For each class

_____ spectrophotometers with instructions (1 per team)
_____ Kimwipes (1 box per spectrophotometer)
_____ *Coleus* plant with multicolored leaves (1)

Supplies in the Hood

For each class

_____ acetone, 250-mL bottle (1)
_____ 10-mL graduated cylinders (3–5)
_____ waste container for discarded acetone/chlorophyll extract solutions

Instructor's Desk

For each class

_____ projection technology (computer with digital projector or document camera, or overhead projector)
_____ computer with Table 6.3 downloaded in Excel format
_____ transparency of Table 6.3 (if computers are not available)
_____ USB drive

Greenhouse Supplies

For each class

_____ *Coleus* with multicolored leaves (12 leaves per plant)
_____ geranium plant (12 leaves per plant)
_____ one flat of bean plants (for chlorophyll extract)
_____ one flat of bean plants for Exercise 6.1 (instead of geraniums)

Grocery Supplies

_____ spinach or other greens (for chlorophyll extract) (equivalent of 1 bunch)

Solutions/Chemicals

For each two students

_____ small beaker of chlorophyll extract (1)
_____ quart jar with chromatography solvent (9 parts petroleum ether : 1 part acetone) (1) (Keep this in the hood.)
_____ wash bottle of DI water (1)
_____ dropper bottle of I_2KI (1)

Mitosis and Meiosis

Students work in pairs in modeling exercises, independently in all other activities.

Instructions for making squashes of cells undergoing mitosis or meiosis in living root tips and anthers are now in the laboratory manual in the Investigative Extensions section of Lab Topic 7. Supplies needed for this activity are included in this chapter of the Preparation Guide. Laboratory instructors may find it helpful to have a photomicroscopy system available to assist students as they locate the best regions on their slides to find chromosomes. Be careful, however, that students observe their own slides and do not rely on the instructor to locate the cells.

For Each Student

- compound microscope
- prepared slide of onion root tip, l.s. (Carolina Biological Supply # 302396, # 302408; Triarch # 14-2b or 14-2c), Exercise 7.2
- prepared slide of whitefish blastulas (Carolina Biological Supply # 308946), Exercise 7.3, Lab Study B
- blank slides and coverslips, Exercise 7.5 (We ask students to supply their own.)

For Each Two Students

- lens paper
- 2 of each letter *B, D, b,* and *d* typed on peel-and-stick mailing labels, Exercise 7.4 (Alternatively, have labeling tape and permanent markers for students to make their own labels.)
- dropper bottle of water, Exercise 7.5

Exercises 7.1 and 7.4

Place the following in plastic self-sealing sandwich bags or pint-sized reusable cups:
- 60 pop beads of one color
- 60 pop beads of a second color
- 8 magnetic centromeres
- 8 centrioles

  The four previous items are available in a kit for a class of 30 (Carolina Biological Supply # 171100), or a kit for two to four students (Carolina Biological Supply # 171110). Individual items may also be purchased, for example, magnetic centromeres (Carolina Biological Supply # 171115). We purchased the kits initially and have since supplemented them with individual items. Centrioles can be made by cutting 1-cm pieces of large-diameter straws.

Demonstration/Supplies Table

- prepared slide of human chromosomes (Carolina Biological Supply # 309140) on a compound microscope, Exercise 7.3, Lab Study A (Oil immersion is preferred but not necessary.)

Exercise 7.5

- 2 petri dishes with cultures of *Sordaria* resulting from a cross between tan strains and wild-type strains
- 2 wire bacterial transfer loops or dissecting needles
- 2 alcohol lamps
- 2 books of matches

  The alcohol lamps and matches are necessary only if you intend to keep the *Sordaria* cultures sterile. If you do not care if cultures become contaminated, you can use the loops, dissecting needles, or even toothpicks to transfer a sample of the *Sordaria* to the microscope slide.

Instructor's Desk

- projection technology (computer with digital projector or document camera, or over-head projector)
- USB drive
- image of the cell cycle downloaded from www.masteringbiology.com.
- transparency showing the cell cycle (Enlarge Figure 7.1 for introductory comments if computers are not available.)
- photomicroscopy system (optional)

Live/Prepared Materials

Sordaria Crosses

Materials:

- petri dish culture of tan *Sordaria fimicola* (Carolina Biological Supply # 156295) We find that tan strains work better than gray strains, although both will work.
- petri dish culture of black, wild-type *Sordaria fimicola* (Carolina Biological Supply # 156291)
- *Sordaria* crossing agar (Carolina Biological Supply # 156354)
- sterile petri dishes size 100 x 10 mm (Carolina Biological Supply # 741248, Fisher Scientific # 08-757-12)
- narrow metal spatula
- alcohol lamp and matches
- wax pencil

Twelve to 14 days before the crosses are to be examined in lab, make the crosses as follows:

1. Pour the crossing agar in sterile petri dishes. The agar comes in small bottles. Loosen the lids of the bottles and heat the bottles with lids in a water bath or in a microwave. If you use a microwave, heat on high for 60-second intervals until the crossing agar is melted. Watch the bottles in the microwave constantly. After each minute, tighten the lid on the bottle and turn the bottle a couple of times. Allow to cool slightly and pour into sterile dishes. One bottle makes about four petri dishes.

2. After the agar has cooled, label the bottom of each petri dish as illustrated:

T = tan, *B* = black (wild type)

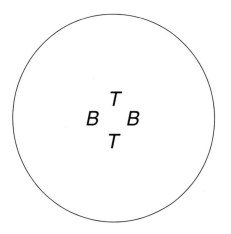

3. Prepare to make the crosses. Using sterile technique, flame the tip end of a narrow metal spatula, and use it to cut 3–4-mm squares of agar from the *tan* culture. Place the squares on the agar over the *T*s in each petri dish. Flame the spatula again and use it to cut squares from the *black, wild-type* culture. Place the squares on the agar over the *B*s in each plate. After the squares have securely adhered to the agar, invert the petri dishes and store them at room temperature until the lab day. After several days your cultures will look like Color Plate 14 in the lab manual. Check the cultures occasionally. When spores are mature you can see them on the inside of the lid as a black film. If spores begin to mature before the lab day, refrigerate the cultures. If cultures begin to dry out, seal them closed with tape or Parafilm.

The greatest number of asci showing crossovers are located at areas of the petri dish indicated by the *X*s in this diagram:

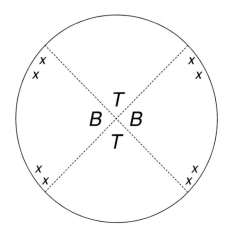

Materials Preparation Notes

Sordaria Crossing Agar

The following recipe is from Jon C. Glase, "A Study of Gene Linkage and Mapping Using Tetrad Analysis in the Fungus *Sordaria fimicola*." *Proceedings of the 16th Workshop/ Conference of the Association for Biology Laboratory Education (ABLE)*, 1994. Dr. Glase says this agar works well and is less expensive than commercially available products.

1. Use 17 g cornmeal agar (Carolina Biological Supply # 742460), 7 g glucose (Sigma-Aldrich # G 8270), 10 g sucrose (Sigma-Aldrich # S 7903), 1 g yeast extract (Carolina Biological Supply # 216746), 0.1 g KH_2PO_4 (Sigma-Aldrich # P 5379), and 1 L water.
2. Autoclave media at 15 psi for 20–30 minutes.
3. Cool slightly and pour into sterile petri dishes.

Preparing Root Tip or Anther Squashes

Allowing students to investigate mitosis and meiosis by making slides of dividing cells using living plants is a relatively easy preparation and adds an interesting activity to this laboratory. Potential questions to investigate and instructions for preparing the slides are included in the Investigative Extensions section of Lab Topic 7 of the laboratory manual. Additional instructions and preparation notes are given below.

Plants for Mitosis

Onion root tips: purchase onion bulbs from a supermarket and trim away any old roots and leaves. Suspend the bulbs on a beaker of water that is slightly larger than the bulb so that the root area remains in the water until the roots begin to grow. If needed, use toothpicks to help suspend the bulb in the water. The roots usually reach the correct size in about 3 to 4 days.

***Tulbaghia violacea* roots:** purchase these plants from nursery supply houses. Maintain the plants in pots in the greenhouse until needed. *T. violacea* chromosomes are fewer ($2n = 10$) and larger than onion chromosomes and produce excellent root tip squashes. When needed, remove the plants from the pots and cut off the youngest, translucent root tips. Gently wash to remove any soil particles.

Plants for Meiosis

Tradescantia sp. and *Tulbaghia violacea* both provide excellent materials for obtaining meiotic figures. These plants are usually available in nursery supply houses, and are easily maintained in a greenhouse. When flowers are beginning to bloom, before the buds open and just as a faint color is visible in petals in the buds (this is the time that meiosis is taking place in anthers), use a dissecting needle to remove the buds to use for anther squashes. Remaining buds may be used on subsequent days.

1 *N* HCl

Add enough DI water to make 120 mL of liquid to 10 mL of concentrated HCl (Carolina Biological Supply # 867790). Keep in dropper bottles.

Acetocarmine Stain

This stain may be purchased commercially (Carolina Biological Supply # 841423). We have never used this, so we cannot vouch for its success.

To prepare your own solution, mix the following:
- 55 mL DI water
- 45 mL acetic acid (Carolina Biological Supply # 841290)
- 0.05 g carmine powder (Sigma-Aldrich # C 1022-5g)

Boil gently for 5 minutes. Shake, cool, and filter.

Staining results may be improved by using an iron dissecting needle to mix the drop of acetocarmine on the slide before adding the root tip.

Reference Materials

A Web search for "mitosis" and then "meiosis" yields several excellent animated and video clips of mitosis and meiosis. These may be used as you introduce the lab topic. Also see media resources and websites listed in the lab manual and at www.masteringbiology.com.

Checklist of Materials

Equipment

For each student

_____ compound microscope (1)
_____ slides (1–2)
_____ glass coverslips (1–2)
                 prepared slides of:
_____   onion root tip (1)
_____   whitefish blastula (1)

For each two students

_____ lens paper (1 package)
_____ dropper bottle of water (1)
_____ pop beads of one color (60)
_____ pop beads of a second color (60)
_____ magnetic centromeres (8)
_____ centrioles (8)
_____ the letters B, D, b, and d typed on mailing labels (2 of each)
_____ self-sealing sandwich bag (1)

Demonstration/Supplies Table

For each class

_____ prepared slide of human chromosomes/compound scope (1)
_____ immersion oil (1)
_____ petri dish cultures of *Sordaria* crosses (2)
_____ wire bacterial loops (2)
_____ alcohol lamps (2)
_____ matches (2)

Instructor's Desk

For each class

_____ projection technology (computer with digital projector or document camera, or overhead projector)
_____ image of the cell cycle in PowerPoint or a transparency (if computers are not available)
_____ video of cell reproduction
_____ photomicroscopy system (optional)

Live/Prepared Materials

Numbers in parentheses are the amounts required for preparation of four plates. Have two plates for each class.

for *Sordaria* crosses:
_____ sterile petri dishes (4)
_____ *Sordaria fimicola* tan culture (1) (One culture can be used to make many crosses.)
_____ *Sordaria fimicola* black (wild-type) culture (1) (One culture can be used to make many crosses.)
_____ *Sordaria* crossing agar (1 bottle for 4 dishes)
_____ narrow metal spatula (1)
_____ alcohol lamp and matches (1)
_____ wax pencil (1)

Reference Materials

_____ videos of mitosis/meiosis (1)

Mendelian Genetics I: Fast Plants

This laboratory project takes 6–8 weeks to complete. Students, working in teams of four, plant their seeds in the first week of the term. The students maintain their own plants, thinning them and checking on water and proper lighting. Students will need precise instructions about where they can find materials and whom to ask for help. We keep materials in a large tray near the plants, and one faculty member or teaching assistant is designated as the contact person. Two weeks after planting, the students will pollinate their plants for the next 5 days or so. Seeds are collected around 39 days, and these seeds are germinated and scored during the following week. These times will vary slightly, but if the plants are maintained in a warm room, with plenty of light and water, they will follow the schedule outlined in General Procedures for All Exercises in the laboratory manual. Also, see Tables 8.2, 8.6, and 8.10. Check the progress of the plants' development, and adjust the laboratory schedule if necessary.

We begin this lab in the first week of the semester before labs have actually begun or during the first week of lab. Students are reminded each week to check their plants, pollinate flowers, or collect seeds. The laboratory period dedicated to this lab can be either week 7 or week 8 of the semester (or quarter). We use week 7 for the lab. In this week the projects are not quite complete, and we use the lab period for a class discussion in which we review crosses and discuss the results to date. We discuss problems that might have affected the results and project a completion date for the project and paper. Since students must pool their data, a date must be set for terminating data collection. In this lab period we review the chi-square test, the required elements for the paper, rules for sharing data (but writing independently), and any other matters of concern. We try not to reveal the explanation of cytoplasmic inheritance for Exercise 8.3 but rather to ask questions and suggest readings that might lead students to this explanation.

If you choose to have the lab period in week 8, use the laboratory time for reporting and discussing final results.

If this is the first time you've tried a continuing laboratory project, you might decide to use only one of the exercises. You will be amazed at how much your students will enjoy this opportunity and how easy Fast Plants are to grow and manipulate for genetic studies. Remember, this is a new experience for the students, too. Warn students that lab is not over in 2 or 3 hours and that the survival of their plants is their responsibility.

For Each Four Students

Materials are organized according to when they will be needed by the student teams during the course of this laboratory project. Please refer to the Schedules of Activities in the lab manual (Tables 8.2, 8.6, and 8.10). Approximate days on which these materials will be needed are provided with the materials list.

- computer with Tables 8.3, 8.4, 8.5, 8.7, 8.8, 8.9, and 8.11 downloaded in Excel format from www.masteringbiology.com in Instructor Resources. Students can record their data and analyze the results.
- USB drive

Planting Seeds and Culture of Plants (Day 1)

- 3 quads
- 12 wicks
- potting mix
- 36 fertilizer pellets
- 1 watering tray with mat
- 3 labels
- 2 permanent markers
- 2 pipettes with bulbs for watering plants
- 1 set of forceps
- dropper bottle of 20% $CuSO_4$ or anti-algae squares
- 12 F_1 seeds (ANL/anl) from a wild type × anthocyaninless (Carolina Biological Supply # 158880), Exercise 8.1
- 12 F_1 seeds (anl/ANL, ygr/YGR) from an anthocyaninless × yellow-green, purple (Carolina Biological Supply # 158890), Exercise 8.2
- Three possible alternative phenotypes are "rosette," "petite," and "astroplants." Use purchased F_1 seeds if available, or make your own crosses and collect F_1 seeds. F_1 seeds of wild type × rosette are available (Carolina Biological Supply # 158884). Crossing these plants produces a 3 normal : 1 rosette ratio. The "petite" mutant (Carolina Biological Supply # 158832) is a recessive allele producing plants 5–15 cm tall. This is not due to the absence of gibberellic acid and could be used with "rosette" to test which strain responds to gibberellic acid. "Astroplants" (Carolina Biological Supply # 158835) is a variety of "petite" with uniform 10-cm plants. These plants were selected for research in space.
- 6 seeds from homozygous green plants (wild type) (Carolina Biological Supply # 158810), Exercise 8.3
- 6 seeds from homozygous variegated plants (var) (Carolina Biological Supply # 158820), Exercise 8.3

Note: The seeds for variegated plants require a couple of extra days to germinate and, therefore, must be planted in advance of the wild-type plants. The lab preparator can plant the variegated seeds in advance for each team, or the students can return to lab on their own and plant the wild type 2 days later.

Pollinating and Seed Collection (Day 14–16)

- 3 index cards (5 in. × 8 in.)
- 12 stakes (small wooden applicator sticks, or use plant label stakes—(Carolina Biological Supply # 158982)
- 6 bee sticks
- 1 set of forceps
- 1 seed collecting pan
- 4 seed envelopes or boxes

Germination of Offspring (Day 39 or so; check the plants.)

- 1 glass petri dish with lid, Exercise 8.1
- 1 piece of filter paper to fit petri dish, Exercise 8.1
- 1 water reservoir (dishes of appropriate size or cut-off base of a 2-L drink bottle; see Figure 8.8 for Exercise 8.1)
- labeling tape
- 1 permanent marker
- 2 quads, Exercises 8.2 and 8.3
- 8 wicks, Exercises 8.2 and 8.3
- potting mix, Exercises 8.2 and 8.3
- 1 watering tray with mat, Exercises 8.2 and 8.3
- 2 labels, Exercises 8.2 and 8.3
- 2 pipettes with bulbs for watering plants, Exercises 8.2 and 8.3
- seeds collected by students from each of the three crosses (The students should have these in their seed boxes.)

On day 39 you may want to germinate seeds of the parental phenotypes. Even though students have seen the phenotypes before beginning the project, they often will have difficulty distinguishing the leaf color (green, yellow-green) and the presence of anthocyanin (purple, not purple) in the four possible combinations.

Some materials in this section should still be available from the initial seed planting. Students can reuse the watering tray, markers, and watering supplies. The quads can be reused if washed and thoroughly rinsed. The wicks and mats can be thoroughly rinsed and reused as well. However, if algae have grown on these, they should be washed in a 10% household bleach solution, thoroughly rinsed, and allowed to dry overnight. The mats and wicks must not retain residual detergents or household bleach.

For Each Class

- fluorescent light bank (Carolina Biological Supply # 158999) (Or see Materials Preparation Notes for suggestions to construct a light bank.)

Demonstration/Supplies Table

- 1 quad of purple stem and petioles (anthocyanin present) *B. rapa* (ANL/ANL) (Carolina Biological Supply # 158810), Exercise 8.1
- 1 quad of anthocyaninless *B. rapa* (anl/anl) (Carolina Biological Supply # 158812), Exercise 8.1
- 1 quad of purple stem and petioles (anthocyanin present) *B. rapa* (ANL/ANL) (Carolina Biological Supply # 158810), Exercise 8.2
- 1 quad of anthocyaninless yellow-green *B. rapa* (anl/anl ygr/ygr) (Carolina Biological Supply # 158842), Exercise 8.2
- 1 quad of variegated *B. rapa* (var/var) (Carolina Biological Supply # 158820), Exercise 8.3

   These should be *mature* plants with flowers and seedpods; therefore, in the optimum situation, these seeds should be started 2–3 weeks before the students plant their first seeds (before the first lab period). However, it is possible to start these seeds 1 week before the first lab period and simply demonstrate the phenotype in the *seedling* stage, since that is what the students are asked to do. We have also planted these at the same time the students plant their first set of seeds and placed them (with prominent labels) with the student plants so that they can compare phenotypes to those of known genotypes. The first time you work with these plants, you probably will find it helpful to have a set of mature plants and a set of seedlings at the same stage as the students'.

Instructor's Desk

- projection technology (computer with digital projector or document camera, or overhead projector)
- Tables 8.3, 8.4, 8.5, 8.7, 8.8, 8.9, and 8.11 downloaded in Excel format from www.masteringbiology.com in Instructor Resources. Students can record their data and analyze the results in Excel.
- USB drive

Solution Preparation Notes

20% $CuSO_4$

Dissolve 20 g of $CuSO_4$ (Carolina Biological Supply # 856562) in 100 mL of DI water. Stir. Add 4–5 drops of this solution to the water in watering trays to prevent algal growth. Alternatively, add one anti-algae square (Carolina Biological Supply # 158979) to the water in the watering tray.

Live/Prepared Materials

The seeds for these investigations are available from Carolina Biological Supply. Seeds can be ordered separately from the planting and growing supplies, or they can be purchased as kits. If you would like to try other phenotypes, contact Carolina Biological Supply for availability and descriptions. Other sources for seeds and materials can be found at http://www.fastplants.org/how_to_order/.

Kits and Supplies for Experiments

The Carolina kits contain everything needed to grow the plants—the seeds, watering system, quads, soil, bee sticks, and more. These are for a class of 32, assuming students work in pairs. You may find it more economical to use items you have on hand or to order individual components. See catalog numbers for individual items listed below.

Exercise 8.1: Carolina Biological Supply # 158770

Exercise 8.2: Carolina Biological Supply # 158774

Exercise 8.3: Carolina Biological Supply # 158796

To order individual components (all numbers are Carolina Biological Supply): quads (# 158960); wicks (# 158978); watering tray (# 158975); mat for watering tray (# 158977); plant label stakes (# 158982); bee sticks (# 158985) or pollination wands (# 158988); potting mix (# 158965 or # 158966); fertilizer pellets sized for Fast Plants (# 158970 or # 158971)

Materials Preparation Notes

The two most important factors for successful growth are maintaining an adequate water supply through the continuous watering system and providing high–light conditions. Temperature and light conditions may affect flowering times. The instructor may need to adjust the laboratory schedule accordingly.

Watering

Our students are required to check on their plants and ensure proper watering. However, we still check the plants on a regular basis to prevent losses due to desiccation. The wick and reservoir mat must make good contact at all times, and the water level in the reservoir should be checked regularly, particularly before weekends.

The watering systems can be ordered from Carolina Biological Supply or can be constructed from materials available locally. The watering tray can be made from cottage cheese cartons, deli containers with tops, or plastic shoe boxes. Cut a small slice out of the rim of the top to allow the mat to extend into the container of water below. The mat and wicks can be cut from Pellon available at fabric stores. Pellon contains sizing and should be thoroughly washed and rinsed in clean water several times to remove any chemicals. Cut the Pellon to fit the top of the watering tray and then extend down into the reservoir of water, providing a continuous water supply. The wicks are thin strips placed in the bottom of the quads, extending through holes in the bottom to make contact with the mat on the watering system. Refer to Figures 8.5 and 8.6 in the lab manual.

Light

The light bank system does *not* require "grow" lights but uses standard cool white bulbs. Note that 4–6 fluorescent bulbs are used in the light bank. (See Figure 8.6 in the laboratory manual.) The light must be maintained 2–3 inches above the growing plants. This can be achieved by adjusting the height of the lights. (Ours are on chains attached by "S" hooks.) Alternatively, if you will be using a light system with fixed lights, then place the plants on risers (inverted trays would work) and lower the plants as they grow. If you do not maintain the light close to the plants, they will initially be leggy and eventually grow into or around the lights, becoming unmanageable. Flowering may also be later, affecting the schedule for lab activities. The lights are kept on 24 hours a day.

The light system can be ordered from Carolina Biological Supply (# 158999) or constructed from materials available locally. We used inexpensive shop lights and wood from a local supplier for our first light support systems. Later, we used lightweight PVC pipe. The *Wisconsin Fast Plants Growing Instructions* includes diagrams of supports that you can use as guidelines.

Plant Light House

When growing smaller numbers of plants, consider the Plant Light House available at Carolina Biological Supply (# 158994). This may be used to grow up to 64 plants in 16 quads. If your class has 24 students and they work in pairs, you could have 12 quads in a light house.

Directions for building a similar lighting box from plastic crates is available at http://www.fastplants.org/how_to_grow/growing_lighting/light_box_system.php.

Quads

Quads (Figure 8.5 in the laboratory manual) are available from Carolina Biological Supply. These are reusable and take up a minimum of space on the water trays. However, the plants can be grown in any small container. Consider using 35-mm film cases, which are available free of charge from film developing businesses. (They are usually discarded by the hundreds.) Use a hot probe or other instrument to make a hole in the bottom that is large enough for a wick to extend through. Four of these would substitute for one quad and can be held together with a wide rubber band. The film cases will require more room.

Potting Soil

Potting soil can be ordered from Carolina Biological Supply (# 158965 or # 158966). If purchased locally, potting soil should not be primarily peat moss. Do not buy soil for African violets. The soil needs to be a fine-textured artificial mix available from garden and greenhouse suppliers. If the soil has large pieces of bark or peat, consider sifting the soil through a screen or chopping it in a heavy-duty blender. Do not dig soil from the garden!

Bee Sticks

Dried bees to make bee sticks are available from Carolina Biological Supply (# 158985). Bee sticks are made using abdomens of dead bees and toothpicks. Dead bees can be collected from beekeepers. A nature center near us has an indoor hive, and when they clean it out, they call us. Separate the head, thorax, wings, legs, and abdomen. Glue the thorax onto toothpicks using high-strength glue. Pollination wands (Carolina Biological Supply # 158988) may be substituted for bee sticks, but making bee sticks is much more interesting!

Reference Materials

We strongly recommend that you purchase the *Fast Plants Growing Instruction Guide* (Carolina Biological Supply # 158952), which includes general background information, instructions for planting, plant care, pollination, and plans for constructing a light bank. Exercises are NOT included in this booklet. For additional exercises using other mutants mentioned in the lab manual see the Wisconsin Fast Plants Information Documents at the Carolina Biological Supply website, http://www.carolina.com/fastplants/.

Wisconsin Fast Plants Manual. 1989. Burlington, NC: Carolina Biological Supply.

Wisconsin Fast Plants also produces a newsletter with helpful information and suggestions. Write to Wisconsin Fast Plants, University of Wisconsin–Madison, Dept. of Plant Pathology, 1630 Linden Dr., Madison, WI 53706. (608) 263-2634. Additional information is available at the website http://www.fastplants.org/.

Checklist of Materials

Equipment

For each class

_____ fluorescent light bank (1–2)
_____ Plant Light House (option for growing smaller numbers of plants)

For each four students

_____ computer with Tables 8.3, 8.4, 8.5, 8.7, 8.8, 8.9, and 8.11 downloaded in Excel format from www.masteringbiology.com
_____ USB drive
_____ quads (5)

_____ wicks (20)
_____ potting mix, 1-lb bag (½–1)
_____ fertilizer pellets (60)
_____ watering tray with mat (1)
_____ labels (6)
_____ permanent markers (1–2)
_____ 5-in. × 8-in. index cards (3)
_____ bee sticks (6)
_____ stakes (12)
_____ forceps (1–2)
_____ pipettes with bulbs (2)
_____ seed collecting pan (1)
_____ seed boxes or envelopes (4)
_____ glass petri dish with lid (1)
_____ filter paper to fit petri dish (1)
_____ water reservoir (1)

Demonstration/Supplies Table

For each class

_____ quads of wild-type plants (2)
_____ quad of anthocyaninless plants (1)
_____ quad of anthocyaninless/yellow-green plants (1)
_____ quad of variegated plants (1)

Instructor's Desk

_____ projection technology (computer with digital projector or document camera, or overhead projector)
_____ Tables 8.3, 8.4, 8.5, 8.7, 8.8, 8.9, and 8.11 downloaded in Excel format from www.masteringbiology.com or transparencies (if computers are not available)
_____ USB drive

Solutions/Chemicals

For each four students

_____ dropper bottle of 20% $CuSO_4$ (1)
_____ anti-algae squares (optional)

Live/Prepared Materials

For each four students

_____ F_1 seeds from a wild type × anthocyaninless (12)
_____ F_1 seeds from a yellow-green purple × anthocyaninless (12)
_____ seeds from homozygous green plants (6)
_____ seeds from homozygous variegated plants (6)

LAB TOPIC 9

Mendelian Genetics II: *Drosophila*

The flies used for this lab topic are available from Carolina Biological Supply (see ordering instructions in the Fly Cultures section) and are a newly created stronger, more reliable strain. If you have never worked with fruit flies before, we suggest that you find someone in your department who can give you suggestions for successfully culturing the flies and making the crosses. That person may be able to help you find the most economic sources for materials or perhaps even share materials such as fly bottles, vials, and etherizers. If you do not have a colleague who can help, purchase a *Drosophila* guide. Become familiar with the life cycle of *Drosophila* before you begin. If you order supplies from Carolina Biological Supply, the company will send you instructions for maintaining and studying *Drosophila*. We suspect that this is true for other biological supply houses as well.

Students perform all exercises in the lab in pairs.

The first time we performed this lab, we worked out the schedule and entered all activities dealing with the fly crosses on a large desk calendar designated for this purpose only. We modify this schedule each year to fit that year's calendar. It is important to remember that fly crosses must be checked regularly—the quality of the medium can vary from year to year, the temperature of the room can vary, and the fly strain can be weak. The success of this lab depends on careful attention to the fly crosses. Many supplies can be used year after year. Only living flies with designated genotypes, the medium to grow the flies, and often the chemicals for the assay mixture must be purchased each year.

With careful planning, this lab is a huge success. The prep is spread out over several weeks; however, during the actual week of the lab, the prep is minimal.

Editions 1–3 of the lab manual included an exercise on the Developmental Profile of the aldox gene. Later editions suggested this activity as an "Investigative Extension." We have included the procedure for performing this investigation, studying the developmental profile of the aldox gene, in this chapter of this Preparation Guide, following the Checklist of Materials.

One of our reviewers, Jane Rasco of the University of Alabama, says that she collects and freezes the flies over several weeks before the lab begins. We have not tried using frozen flies, but this sounds like a good idea. We would suggest freezing the flies at –80°C if possible, to keep the enzymes active.

BioQUEST's "Genetics Construction Kit" is an excellent software-based program that mates *Drosophila*-like organisms simulating transmission genetics. We suggest this program as a possible investigative extension of this lab topic. For information see http://bioquest.org/BQLibrary/library_result.php. From the list of library modules, select Genetics Construction Kit. You may then preview the software manual and download the complete module.

For Each Two Students

- stereoscopic microscope
- dropper bottle of ether or FlyNap

60

- 1 3-in. × 5-in. index card (used to carry flies)
- 1 4-in. × 6-in. index card (to cover spot plates)
- toothpick or small watercolor paintbrush (used to manipulate flies)
- re-etherizer (petri dish with gauze pad taped in lid)
- 2 spot assay test plates with 48 or 96 wells

We use white plastic test plates, approximate dimensions 19 cm × 28 cm, with 96 depressions (the same used for Lab Topic 4 Enzymes). In recent years we have had difficulty locating a supplier for the white plates, but clear plastic plates are available from Fisher Scientific, # 07-200-86 (48 wells) or # 07-200-88 (96 wells). If you use clear plates, have students place them over a piece of white paper to be able to see the assay mixture color change. We do not allow the students to write on the plates. It is impossible to remove marks. Write labels on a piece of paper beside the plate. Warn students to wash the plates carefully after they have finished each experiment. They are impossible to clean after they have dried soiled. We have tried to clean them with a bleach solution with limited success.

- dropper bottle with about 10 mL of assay mixture
- disposable gloves for use with assay mixture
- paper towels
- pestle
- Kimwipes
- wash bottle of DI water (to rinse spot plates if a sink is not available)
- fly vial 1a, Exercises 9.1, 9.2, 9.3, and 9.4
- fly vial 1b, Exercise 9.1
- fly vial 2, Exercise 9.2
- fly vial 3, Exercise 9.3
- fly vial 4, Exercise 9.4

For Each Four Students

- computers with Tables 9.4, 9.5, and 9.7 downloaded in Excel format from www.masteringbiology.com. Students should select Study Area, Lab Media, Investigating Biology Lab Data Tables—9th edition. Instructors go to Instructor Resources, Instructor Guides for Supplements, and then Data Tables from Investigating Biology Lab Manual, 9e. Students can record their data and analyze the results. You may request that students have a USB drive to record their results.

Instructor's Desk

- projection technology (computer with digital projector or document camera, or overhead projector)
- If computers are not available for each four students, then have Tables 9.4, 9.5, and 9.7 downloaded in Excel format from www.masteringbiology.com in Instructor Resources. Students can record their data and analyze the results.
- USB drive to record final class data.
- Have available PowerPoint slides, scanned images, or transparencies of:

  1. Worksheets for Naming Genes, Exercise 9.2.
     At the end of this chapter (pp. 68–70), we have included three masters for the lab instructor to use to lead a class discussion on the conventional way to name genes in *Drosophila* genetics. Use the first image (p. 68) to introduce the conventional way to name the gene. Use the second (p. 69) to lead students to predict all possible results of the cross in Exercise 9.2. Depending on the results, students will be able to predict the inheritance of the gene and tell how to name the gene in

each case. We make paper copies of this sheet and give one to each student to fill in as the class discussion takes place. The third master (p. 70) describes the correct answers and is for the instructor only.

2. If computers are not available, provide a Class Data Sheet for Exercise 9.3 using the master p. 71, Table 9.4. Use this to record the total class data so students can perform the chi-square test in their lab manuals, Table 9.5.

3. If computers are not available, provide a Class Data Sheet for Exercise 9.4 using the master p. 72, Table 9.7. Use this to record the total class data so students can perform the chi-square test on separate paper. Typical results are given in the laboratory manual.

Solution Preparation Notes

Ether or FlyNap

Ether can be purchased from any chemical/biological supply house. FlyNap, Carolina Biological Supply # 173010, can be substituted for ether. Remember that ethyl ether fumes are explosive. Use in a well-ventilated room. Inhale as little as possible. Do not use around flames or sparks! For our preparation room, rather than ether, we order a small canister of carbon dioxide to use to put the flies to sleep. We made a "sleep chamber" out of a plastic bottle. Check with a geneticist in your department about using CO_2 and "sleep chambers."

Assay Mixture

500 mL is enough for four labs of 24 students each (or 125 mL per lab).

Prepare fresh assay mixture daily. If there is leftover mixture, refrigerate the excess and check to see if it is still good the next day by checking the color. If the mixture is yellowish, it is okay to use the second day. If it is bluish, discard. Store the assay mixture in dark bottles. Just before lab, dispense about 10 mL into small labeled amber dropper bottles, used only for this mixture (save and use year after year).

> NBT = nitroblue tetrazolium, Sigma-Aldrich # N 6876—store at 2–8°C
> PMS = phenazine methosulfate, Sigma-Aldrich # P 9625—store at 0°C
> AN = anisaldehyde, Sigma-Aldrich # A 0519—store in the hood
> TRIS = TRIZMA BASE, Sigma-Aldrich # T 1503, Fisher Scientific # BP152

To prepare the assay mixture:

Per 100 mL	Per 500 mL
25 mg (0.025 g) NBT	125 mg (0.125 g) NBT
2 mg (0.002 g) PMS	10 mg (0.010 g) PMS
150 microliters AN (1 drop)	0.75 mL AN (7–10 drops)
100 mL 0.1 M TRIS (pH 8)*	50 mL (1 M) TRIS (pH 8)
—	DI water to 500 mL

*Note that the 1 M TRIS must be diluted to make 100 mL of assay.

1 M TRIS (pH 8)

1. Dissolve 121.14 g TRIS in 700 mL DI water.
2. Add HCl drop by drop until the pH is 8.0. Expect to add several drops.
3. Add DI water to make 1 L.

To make 100 mL of **0.1 *M* TRIS,** dissolve 1.2 g TRIS in 70 mL DI water. Adjust the pH, then increase the volume to 100 mL with DI water.

The pH of the solution is very important. If the pH is not exactly 8, the assay mixture will quickly turn blue and be useless.

> The assay mixture contains carcinogens. Do not allow it to contact the skin. Use disposable gloves to prepare the assay mixture, and wash hands thoroughly afterward. If contact is made with the skin, wash the area thoroughly using soap and water. In the event of a spill, wipe up the liquid with dry towels and wash the area thoroughly using soap, water, and disposable towels. Dispose of all towels and gloves in a plastic bag in the trash.

Live/Prepared Materials

Fly Cultures

This list includes the individual items you will need for culturing flies. We suggest that you look through the items available from Carolina Biological Supply or other suppliers for your particular needs. You may choose to order kits or sets.

- 240-mL (about ½-pt) *Drosophila* culture bottles (Carolina Biological Supply # 173135)
- 1¼-in.-diameter, 4-in.-high *Drosophila* culture vials (Carolina Biological Supply # 173120)
- *Drosophila* vial plugs (Carolina Biological Supply # 173122) (Balls of cotton are cheaper and can be substituted for these foam plugs, but the foam plugs are easier to use.)
- cotton or foam plugs to fit bottles (Carolina Biological Supply uses the same plugs for both vials and bottles.)
- fly medium (Carolina Biological Supply # 173200) (an instant medium, or you can make your own)
- *Drosophila* stocks
- wild-type flies (Carolina Biological Supply # 172100)
- sepia aldox mutants (chromosome 3) For ordering information, see the note below.

> Carolina Biological Supply is the only supplier for the sepia aldox mutant strain of *Drosophila*; however, this mutant is not listed in the catalog. You can order these flies from the Carolina website using the number **172582**, or by telephone. Call Carolina at 1-800-334-5551. Order the flies using the same number (172582). Confirm that this is the strain you are ordering (sepia lpo aldox) with the person taking the order. If you have problems placing the order, call the *Drosophila* lab at extension 5424.

If you do not intend to perform Exercise 9.4, Mapping Genes, you may substitute rosy aldox (rosy lpo/aldox, Carolina Biological Supply # 172561). This strain of flies gives excellent results for the AO enzyme assay test, and can be substituted for sepia aldox in Exercises 9.1, 9.2, and 9.3. *However, if you plan to perform Exercise 9.4, Mapping Genes, the rosy aldox genotype cannot be used.* The rosy gene is located on the same chromosome as aldox and sepia (chromosome 3) but is very close to the aldox gene. Consequently, the frequency of crossovers and recombinant classes will be very rare and virtually undetected by students.

Obtain the flies and begin expanding the stock at least 3 months before the day of the lab. Carolina Biological Supply requests that you order flies 2 weeks before you will begin to expand your stocks.

Fly Vials

You will be preparing five different vials of flies:

- vial 1a: **aldox⁺ aldox⁺** (wild type, enzyme present) flies, about 10 males and 10 females
- vial 1b: **aldox aldox** (lack the AO enzyme) flies, about 5 males and 5 females
- vial 2: at least 20 F₁ flies from a cross between a homozygous **aldox aldox** (*sepia lpo aldox* mutant) female and a homozygous **aldox⁺ aldox⁺** (wild-type) male, 10 males and 10 females

  If circumstances require it, you may substitute all wild-type flies for this vial because you know that the flies resulting from this cross will all have the enzyme present.
- vial 3: at least 24 flies from a mating between 2 heterozygotes, **aldox⁺ aldox.**
- vial 4: 50 F₁ flies from a dihybrid test cross between a parent that is heterozygous for both traits, **sepia⁺ aldox⁺/sepia aldox** and a parent that is homozygous recessive for both traits, **sepia aldox/sepia aldox.**

Calendar for Preparing Fly Crosses

(We have a large desk calendar used exclusively to record dates and activities for preparing the fly crosses.)

3 Months Before Lab

When the original cultures arrive, transfer the adults to labeled and dated bottles, one (or more if flies are plentiful) per strain. Give the flies 4–5 days to lay eggs, and transfer the parents to additional bottles. Continue transferring flies to new bottles about once every week. Watch the cultures to be sure they are healthy.

The life cycle of the fly consists of development from the fertilized egg to larva, to a pupal stage, to the adult fly. The egg-larval stage at 25°C is about 5 days. At 20°C it is about 8 days. The pupal stage is 4.2 days at 25°C and 6.3 days at 20°C. Thus, at 25°C the life cycle from fertilized egg to adult fly is about 10 days, and at 20°C it is about 15 days.

6–7 Weeks Before Lab

Collect virgin females of each phenotype. This will take several days. Save males separately to use for reciprocal crosses.

There are two methods for virgin collection. The traditional method is to keep flies at room temperature and collect every 8–10 hours before emerging flies mate. An alternate method, however, is based on the principle that females emerging in jars lacking old adult males will not mate with their young brothers for 24 hours if kept at 16–18°C. Therefore, when collecting, an easy schedule is as follows:

On Day 1, as soon as pupae darken, clear jars of all adults and place at 18°C. Collect virgin females the next morning, leave at room temperature or 25°C for 8 hours, collect again, and leave overnight at 18°C. If you want to collect only once per 24 hours, first clear and then keep the cultures at 16–18°C.

5 Weeks Before Lab

Make the cross **sepia⁺ aldox⁺/sepia⁺ aldox⁺ × sepia aldox/sepia aldox** (or, in other words, cross the wild type with the mutant). This produces the heterozygotes for later crosses. Be sure to keep both parent stocks at a reasonable level as they will be used to produce vials 1a and 1b, and the mutants will be crossed with heterozygotes to produce vial 4.

3–4 Weeks Before Lab

1. Discard the parents of the cross made at 5 weeks and begin to collect virgin flies (heterozygotes) for the vial 4 cross.
2. After sufficient numbers of virgin females (heterozygotes) have been collected to make the cross for vial 4, transfer the remaining heterozygotes to fresh media and allow them to mate to produce vial 3.
3. Collect virgin females from the original mutant (**aldox aldox**; lacking the enzyme) cultures and cross with males from the original wild-type cultures to produce vial 2. The reciprocal of this cross will work as well. Since this vial will show all positive offspring, as suggested before, in an emergency you can substitute flies from the wild-type cultures for this vial.

2½–3 Weeks Before Lab

Make the cross for vial 4. Cross the heterozygote virgin females previously collected with the homozygous-recessive males. We make this cross in small vials with fly medium. After eggs or larvae are visible, transfer the parents to new vials to increase the number of vials.

Day of Lab (or Day Before Lab)

Prepare one vial 1a and one vial 1b for each two students. Etherize flies in one mutant and one wild-type stock bottle. Transfer the designated number of wild-type flies to empty vials and label each appropriately (1a or 1b). If you keep these flies for only a day or so, these vials do not need to have fly medium.

Materials Preparation Notes

Re-Etherizer

Tape a gauze pad in the lid of a petri dish. Saturate the gauze pad with ether and place this pad over the flies should any begin to awaken while you are working with them.

Making the Pestles

The purpose of the pestle is to mash flies in the assay mixture in spot plate wells. Use a small glass pestle with a bulb at one end. We made our pestles from glass rods, diameter about 0.5 cm, cut in 8–10-cm lengths. Choose a glass rod with a diameter that easily fits the wells in your spot plates. You may prepare the pestles as follows:

1. Wearing fire-resistant gloves and using a Bunsen burner, heat one end of the rod until it has no sharp edges.
2. Cool completely.
3. Heat the other end and press the hot end against a burn-proof (asbestos) surface to make a slightly larger, rounded bulblike end.
4. Cool completely before touching.

Checklist of Materials

Equipment

For each two students

_____ stereoscopic microscope (1)
_____ small index cards (3 in. × 5 in.) (2)
_____ large index cards (4 in. × 6 in.) (2)
_____ toothpicks or paintbrushes (2)
_____ paper towels, stack (1)
_____ pestle (1)
_____ Kimwipes (1 box)
_____ re-etherizer (1)
_____ spot assay plates (2)

For each four students

_____ computer with Tables 9.4, 9.5, and 9.7 downloaded in Excel format from www.masteringbiology.com
_____ USB drive

For each class

_____ disposable gloves (1 box)

Instructor's Desk

For each class

_____ projection technology (computer with digital projector or document camera, or overhead projector)
_____ Tables 9.4, 9.5, and 9.7 downloaded in Excel format from www.masteringbiology.com
_____ USB drive
scanned images or transparencies of:
_____ Worksheet for Naming Genes, Exercise 9.2 (2 sheets, 1 of each for students, plus Worksheet 3, For Instructor Only)
_____ Table 9.4 Class Data Sheet, Exercise 9.3 (1)
_____ Table 9.7 Class Data Sheet, Exercise 9.4 (1)

Solutions/Chemicals

For each two students

dropper bottles of:
_____ ether or FlyNap (1)
_____ assay mixture (1)
_____ wash bottle of DI water (1)

Live/Prepared Materials

For each two students

_____ fly vials: 1a, 1b, 2, 3, 4 (1 each)

Procedure for Developmental Profile of the Aldox Gene in *Drosophila*

(Investigative Extension #1 in *Investigating Biology*)

Materials

- large, active culture bottles of wild-type flies (These can be from your stocks, or students can use vial 1a from the laboratory exercise.)
- remaining materials from Exercise 9.1 (see the exercise in the lab manual)

Introduction

All genes are not active in all cells, nor are genes in a cell lineage active at all times in the developmental cycle of the organism. Cells constantly turn genes on and off, bringing about the patterns of development and differentiation in the organism.

There are four distinct developmental stages in the fruit fly: the embryo, larva, pupa, and adult. The embryo hatches to a larva that undergoes two molts (sheds its skin as it grows) and develops into a non-motile pupa. In the pupal stage, the larval tissues differentiate into adult tissues. Some genes are continuously active in all four stages of development. Others are active at a variety of different times. Still others are active only in one stage. For example, genes controlling the development of adult structures, such as wings, would be active only in the pupal stage. As the pupal stage is completed, the pupal case erupts and the winged fly emerges.

This experiment investigates the expression of the aldox gene during the developmental cycle of the fruit fly. Students perform the assay test on larvae, pupae, and adults, comparing the level of AO in all three stages.

Procedure

1. Anesthetize the flies in the vial or culture bottle.
2. Select five large larvae, five pupae (not the clear, empty pupal cases), and five adult flies.
3. Put each developmental stage in a separate row on the spot plate.
4. Perform the spot assay *simultaneously* on all stages.
5. After 5 minutes, compare the degree of coloration of the various assays. Select the darkest stage and assign it an arbitrary value of 10. Then assign values for the other two stages relative to 10.
6. Ask students to create a graph showing AO activity relative to the stage of development.

Students will find that AO activity is greatest in adults, less in larvae, and least in pupae.

Worksheet 1 for Naming Genes, Exercise 9.2

When naming genes:

Name the gene related to its activity: aldox

Mutant dominant—capitalize name: Aldox

Mutant recessive—lowercase name: aldox

Wild type designated by a superscript +

Cross

FEMALE—enzyme activity absent

MALE—enzyme activity present (wild type)

Possible Names of Parents

1. Mutant dominant, gene is sex-linked

    FEMALE: Aldox Aldox
    MALE: $Aldox^+$ Y

2. Mutant dominant, gene is not sex-linked

    FEMALE: Aldox Aldox
    MALE: $Aldox^+$ $Aldox^+$

3. Mutant recessive, gene is sex-linked

    FEMALE: aldox aldox
    MALE: $aldox^+$ Y

4. Mutant recessive, gene is not sex-linked

    FEMALE: aldox aldox
    MALE: $aldox^+$ $aldox^+$

Worksheet 2 for Naming Genes, Exercise 9.2

Given information: The cross is between a female that has no enzyme (the mutant trait) and a male that has the enzyme (wild type).

Give the gene an appropriate name:

If the mutant is dominant, capitalize the name of the gene.

If the mutant is recessive, use a lowercase letter.

Four Possible Crosses and the Predicted Offspring Ratio

1. Mutant dominant, gene is sex-linked

2. Mutant dominant, gene is not sex-linked

3. Mutant recessive, gene is sex-linked

4. Mutant recessive, gene is not sex-linked

Worksheet 3 for Naming Genes, Exercise 9.2
For Instructor Only

Given information: The cross is between a female that has no enzyme (the mutant trait) and a male that has the enzyme (wild type).

Give the gene an appropriate name (aldox). Students will determine the name at the end of the activity.

If the mutant is dominant, capitalize the name of the gene.

If the mutant is recessive, use a lowercase letter.

Four Possible Crosses and the Predicted Offspring Ratio

1. Mutant dominant, gene is sex-linked

$$Aldox\ Aldox \times Aldox^+\ Y$$

	Aldox⁺	Y
Aldox	no enzyme	no enzyme
Aldox	no enzyme	no enzyme

Results of the cross: none of the offspring will have the enzyme.

2. Mutant dominant, gene is not sex-linked

$$Aldox\ Aldox \times Aldox^+\ Aldox^+$$

	Aldox⁺	Aldox⁺
Aldox	no enzyme	no enzyme
Aldox	no enzyme	no enzyme

Results of the cross: none of the offspring will have the enzyme.

3. Mutant recessive, gene is sex-linked

$$aldox\ aldox \times aldox^+\ Y$$

	aldox⁺	Y
aldox	female, enzyme present	male, enzyme absent
aldox	female, enzyme present	male, enzyme absent

Results of the cross: females have the enzyme, males do not.

4. Mutant recessive, gene is not sex-linked

$$aldox\ aldox \times aldox^+\ aldox^+$$

	aldox⁺	aldox⁺
aldox	enzyme present	enzyme present
aldox	enzyme present	enzyme present

Results of the cross: all offspring will have the enzyme.

After they work through these crosses, have the students predict the results and perform the experiment.

Table 9.4 Class Data Sheet, Exercise 9.3

Record Team Totals in Each Phenotype Category

Team	AO Present	AO Absent
1		
2		
3		
4		
5		
6		
7		
8		
9		
10		
11		
12		
Total		

Ratio of AO Present to AO Absent: _____

Table 9.7 Class Data Sheet, Exercise 9.4

Record Number of Organisms with Each Phenotype

Team	Red Eyes, AO Present	Red Eyes, AO Absent	Sepia Eyes, AO Present	Sepia Eyes, AO Absent
1				
2				
3				
4				
5				
6				
7				
8				
9				
10				
11				
12				
Total				

Molecular Biology

New in this edition, we have updated the procedures for staining and visualizing the gels to use SYBR® Safe, a stain that poses little or no hazard to students and uses a blue light illuminator (rather than UV light). The procedures for staining with methylene blue are provided as an alternative. If you choose to use ethidium bromide, you will need to refer to a previous edition of the laboratory manual. We have included information for a couple of blue light illuminators with a range of features and prices.

Catalog numbers have been supplied for Carolina Biological Supply and New England BioLabs, but other suppliers will have comparable materials and equipment. We purchased our gel systems (# 3487-0000) from USA Scientific and Owl Separation Systems (# 27372-200) from VWR (see Appendix for contact information). Kits with DNA, restriction enzymes, markers, and other supplies are available from several vendors, including Carolina Biological and EDVOTEK. Kits drastically reduce ordering and preparation times; however, they are expensive to use in large introductory biology classes with multiple laboratory sections. They are particularly useful for classes with fewer lab sections and laboratories using molecular techniques for the first time. Suppliers of materials for the exercises in this lab, in addition to Carolina Biological Supply and New England BioLabs, include:

EDVOTEK, Inc., FOTODYNE, Modern Biology, Inc., and Ward's Natural Science. See contact information for vendors in the Appendix.

Because we have found methylene blue stain to be satisfactory and safe, we give prep instructions for this stain as well.

We strongly recommend *DNA Science* by Micklos and Freyer and *Molecular Cloning: A Lab Manual* by Sambrook et al. as references for this laboratory. Other references are included in the lab manual.

For Each Four Students

Exercise 10.1

- gel electrophoresis apparatus consisting of:
  electrophoresis chamber with safety cover (e.g., USA Scientific #3487-0000)
  power supply with electrodes in the range of 50–120 V (e.g., Thermo Scientific Owl ED-105 Compact Power Supply or Carolina NG Electrophoresis Power Supply # 213704)
  gel holder (gel plates)
  comb to make wells
- enough 1× TAE buffer to fill gel chamber and cover the gel

- metric rulers
- wash bottle of DI water
- practice gel in covered petri dish
- colored glycerine water in small beaker (for practicing pipetting)
- empty microtubes (for practicing pipetting)
- beaker for disposing of used microtips
- micropipettors (P20) (Carolina Biological Supply # 214670) and pipette tips (Carolina Biological Supply # 214717) or microcapillary pipettes (Carolina Biological Supply # 214500)
- fine permanent marker
- lab bench liner (Fisher # 14-127-47) taped to an area used for electrophoresis for ease of clean up (optional)
- For each group of four students, prepare the following microtubes, color-coded and containing the listed solutions. (Microtubes—purchase various colors: Fisher #s 05-406-16, 05-406-17, etc.) Students will label the tubes "A," "P," and "AP," as indicated. Buffers are supplied with the enzymes by the vendor.
- Note that 27 μl of water and buffer are added to tubes by the instructor. The tubes will have a final volume of 30 μl. Students add only 20 μl to wells.

Tube label/color (final well #)	Instructor adds	Student will add in lab before incubating tube
A/ _____ (3)	24 μl DI water 3 μl *Ava* II buffer	2 μl pUC19 DNA** 1 μl *Ava* II enzyme
P/ _____ (4)	24 μl DI water 3 μl *Pvu* II buffer	2 μl pUC19 DNA** 1 μl *Pvu* II enzyme
AP/_____ (5)	23 μl DI water 3 μl *Ava* II* buffer	2 μl pUC19 DNA** 1 μl *Ava* II enzyme 1 μl *Pvu* II enzyme

*Use the *Ava* II buffer only.
**The DNA concentration should be 0.5 μg/μl

- Additional microtubes
  - Microtube with gel loading dye (bromophenol blue; Carolina Biological Supply # 218200)
  - Microtube labeled #1 containing 20 mL DI water (for the loading dye for well #1)
  - Microtube labeled #6 containing 18 mL DI water (for uncut pUC19 DNA for well #6)

In summary, each group of four students will have a total of 6 microtubes (A, P, AP, gel loading dye, tube #1, and tube #6). These should be at their work area before the lab begins. Since the contents of the tubes do not need to be refrigerated, they may remain at room temperature. These tubes should be color coded or labeled. Note that tube #2 with the lambda DNA (the molecular weight markers) is in the cold box on the demonstration table. If you are using the additional low molecular weight 200 bp markers, then tube #7 with the markers should also be in the cold box on the demonstration table.

To organize the microtubes, place a small microtube holder at each group's work area. We made our own holders using Styrofoam boxes into which we punched holes with a hot glass rod.

Demonstration/Supplies Table

Exercise 10.1

- Nalgene™ Labtop Cooler (Thermo Scientific #G5115-0032) (An ice chest with ice may be substituted, but is less convenient.)
  In this cooler place the following:
  - one microtube labeled #2 containing 2 μl of lambda DNA markers and 18 μl of DI water *for each group of four students.* The lambda DNA is digested with *Hind* III (New England BioLabs # R0104T, Carolina Biological Supply # 211473).
  - one microtube containing enough pUC 19 DNA (the plasmid) for the entire class (New England BioLabs # N3041S). Students will add 2 μl of this DNA to their tubes A, P, AP, and #6 (total of 8 μl).
  - one microtube containing enough *Ava* II enzyme for the entire class (New England BioLabs # R0153S). Students will add 1 μl of this enzyme to each of their tubes A and AP.
  - one microtube containing enough *Pvu* II enzyme for the entire class (New England BioLabs # R0151S). Students will add 1 μl of this enzyme to each of their tubes P and AP.
  - *optional tube*—one microtube labeled #7 containing 2 μl of lambda DNA markers and 18 μl of DI water *for each group of four students.* These low molecular weight markers (200 bp DNA ladder) come with loading dye already added (New England BioLabs # B7025).
- disposable gloves (box)
- water bath at 37°C for incubation
- tray in water bath to hold microtubes
- water bath at 55°C for melted agarose (if instructor mixes agarose for gels)
- thermometer at each water bath
- one flask with 100 mL of 0.8% agarose containing SYBR® Safe for each team of four students (Note: if using methylene blue omit SYBR® Safe in agarose)
- microwave or hot plate (if students make gels)
- Digital camera to photograph stained gels
- for SYBR® Safe:
  - blue light transilluminator (two suggestions follow):
    Blue Digital Imaging System (Vernier # BL-DBS), includes blue light transilluminator, hood, digital camera and can be connected to Vernier LabPro System. Components can be purchased separately (Blue View Transilluminator only, Vernier # BLUE-VIEW)
    SmartDoc™ Gel Imaging System (Thomas Scientific # 1177X51) uses your smartphone or digital camera to take photos
  - tray for transporting gels to imager (32 oz rectangular Rubbermaid "Take Alongs" or molded plastic sandwich holders work well)
  - waste disposal container for gels
  - disposable gloves
- for methylene blue stain (an alternative to SYBR® Safe):
  - 0.025% methylene blue (or other methylene blue stain—see Solution Preparation Notes)
  - staining trays (32 oz rectangular Rubbermaid "Take Alongs" or molded plastic sandwich holders work well)
  - white light transilluminator (e.g., see New England BioGroup, address in Appendix)
  - DI or distilled water for destaining

> ☣ Check with your chemical safety officer for proper disposal of gels and
> other waste materials.

Solution Preparation Notes

The volumes described here are more than enough for a class of 30 students, unless otherwise indicated.

SYBR® Safe Stain, Exercise 10.1

SYBR® Safe DNA Stain (Fisher #S33102) is supplied as a 10,000× concentration in DMSO. The stain is added to the gel at this concentration and does not need to be diluted. Store at room temperature in the original container. You will add 10 microliters of the stain to 100 mL of gel when you prepare the agarose.

0.025% Methylene Blue, Exercise 10.1 (Alternative Staining Method)

To make 100 mL of stain, add 0.025 g methylene blue powder (Carolina Biological # 875684) to 100 mL DI water. Stir to mix. Depending on the size of your staining trays, make approximately 200 mL stain per gel. You need enough to completely cover the gel.

We have also successfully used DNA InstaStain™ Blue available from EDVOTEK (EDVOTEK # 2003 for 40 gels). This staining procedure uses 7-cm× 7-cm staining papers that are placed directly on the gel. The gel stains in 15 minutes. The disadvantage of using the staining papers is that they can be used only once or twice, whereas the liquid stains may be used repeatedly.

TAE (Tris-acetic, EDTA), Exercise 10.1

Prepare this solution at 10× the concentration needed for the experiment.

To prepare 1 L of 10× TAE:
    48.4 g Tris base (Fisher Scientific # BP152, Sigma-Aldrich # T 1503)
    11.4 mL glacial acetic acid (Fisher Scientific #A38-212)
    3.7 g EDTA (Fisher Scientific # BP118)

Dissolve the Tris, glacial acetic acid and EDTA in 800 mL of DI water and stir until dissolved. Then add DI water up to 1000 mL. Store at room temperature.

To prepare 1 L of 1× TAE:
On the day you will use it, add 100 mL of 10× TAE to 900 mL DI water and stir well. (1× TAE can be reused 2-3 times for running the gels.) Prepare 1× TAE to use in the running chamber, to prepare agarose gels, and to dilute the pUC19 DNA. When diluting pUC19 DNA, use 1× TAE adjusted to pH 8.0. Sterilize the 1× TAE before diluting the DNA by heating it just to boil in a microwave and then allowing it to cool. Watch carefully that the solution does not boil over.

A ready-made solution of TAE may be purchased from EDVOTEK (50× concentration #607) or Sigma Aldrich (10× concentration #T9650).

You may use TBE buffer rather than TAE. A premixed powder of TBE is also available (Fisher Scientific #BP1396-86; EDVOTEK #607-1).

Agarose Gels, Exercise 10.1

We recommend that you prepare agarose for the entire class and keep it warm as directed. Multiply these directions by the number of student teams.

1. To prepare one gel for each student team, put 0.8 g agarose in a 250-mL Erlenmeyer flask and add 100 mL of 1× Tris-acetic EDTA buffer (TAE) (remember to dilute the buffer, if it is not 1×). Check the volume of agarose needed for your gel trays. Some trays hold only 75 mL of agarose.
2. Cover the flask loosely with aluminum foil and heat it on a hot plate with constant stirring (or heat uncovered in a microwave for 2–3 minutes) until the solution begins to boil and is clear (which indicates that all of the agarose is dissolved). If using the microwave, watch carefully. Wearing a heat-resistant glove, remove and swirl the flask.
3. Remove agarose solution from hot plate or microwave. If using the SYBR® Safe stain (Fisher #S33102), add 10 microliters of SYBR® Safe DNA gel stain per 100 mL of gel. Swirl flask until the SYBR® Safe is evenly dispersed throughout the solution. If using the alternative methylene blue stain, do not add any stain to the agarose.
4. Dispense enough liquid agarose for one gel into a flask, one per student team. Keep the flasks in the 55°C water bath in the lab until it is time for students to pour the gels.
5. If you intend to pour the gels rather than have the students do so, allow the solution to cool to a temperature that you can handle with bare hands before pouring the gels. Set the comb over the gel tray so that the teeth rest just above the plate. Slowly pour the gel onto the plate until the solution covers about one-half of the comb's teeth. Avoid bubbles. If any form, quickly and carefully pop them with a micropipette tip. The gel will be opaque when it solidifies. When the gel has hardened, the comb can be removed by squirting some water around the comb and gently pulling the teeth from the gel. Do not pull too fast or the suction will break the bottom of the wells. Wrap the gel in plastic wrap if it is not to be used immediately.

Practice Gels, Exercise 10.1

Add 5 g agar (do not use agarose or nutrient agar) to 500 mL H_2O (this should be enough for 6 gels). Stir and heat until the solution is clear. Pour into gel trays with combs (alternatively, pour into petri dishes in which one or two combs have been positioned). When the agar has solidified, squirt water on the gel and carefully remove the comb. Transfer each gel or a portion of a gel with a row of wells to a petri dish, cover, and store in a refrigerator. These may be prepared several days in advance.

Colored Glycerine Water, Exercise 10.1

This will be used for practice pipetting. Mix 2 parts water, 1 part glycerol (Carolina Biological Supply # 865534), and several drops of methylene blue solution. The mix should be blue enough that students can see it descend into the well as they practice pipetting.

Stocks for the Digestion, Exercise 10.1

Enzymes

Each student group will use 2 μl of *Ava* II enzyme and 2 μl of *Pvu* II enzyme. They will use 4 μl of *Ava* buffer and 2 μl of *Pvu* buffer.

You may use the enzymes in the concentration supplied by the vendor. This may mean that the 1 µl added by students to the respective tubes will contain more enzyme than is needed, but this does not affect the results. Check the labels on your enzymes. Remember that 1 unit of enzyme will digest 1 µg of DNA in 1 hour. The amount of DNA to be digested should be 1 µg (see following prep note). If you choose, you may dilute and adjust the volumes of enzyme so that students add only 1 unit of enzyme.

pUC19 DNA

Before you begin preparing the DNA, check the concentration of your stock. Each digest prepared by the students should contain 1 µg of DNA. The laboratory exercise instructs students to add 2 µl of DNA to each digest and to tube #6. This amount should contain 1 µg of DNA. If the concentration is 1000 µg/mL, this means that 1 µl contains 1 µg. Therefore, if students will add 2 µl to each digest, you will need to make a 0.5 µg/µl solution. To do this, dilute the DNA 1:1 with sterilized 1× TAE or, alternatively, instruct students to add only 1 µl of DNA to tubes A, P, AP, and #6 (the uncut DNA tube).

Keep all tubes with enzymes and DNA on ice or in the cold box until used!

Restriction Buffers, Exercise 10.1

Restriction enzyme buffers are shipped with the enzyme. Check concentrations and dilute if appropriate.

Molecular Weight Markers, Exercise 10.1

Students are asked to add 2 µl of loading dye (bromphenol blue) to the DNA molecular weight markers in microtube 2 just before loading the gel. These microtubes will be at the instructor's desk or demonstration table on ice or in the labtop cooler. We suggest that you run a practice gel with your markers following the directions in the lab manual before the first lab. If you do not get a good separation of marker bands, try preparing the markers by heating them in a 65°C water bath for 5 minutes to melt the annealed ends of the DNA fragments. After this step, dispense the markers into students' microtubes and keep them on ice until used by the students.

We suggest that you add a second set of low molecular weight markers (200 bp DNA ladder, EDVOTEK #756) as tube #7 to assist with identifying the smallest fragments. These often come with the loading dye already added. Include information for the instructor and students for the additional tube.

Gel Loading Dye (Bromophenol Blue), Exercise 10.1

Students add this dye directly to each microtube to verify the movement of the current. (This dye mix does not stain the DNA.) Dissolve the following in enough DI water to make 100 mL:

    50 g sucrose
    0.25 g bromphenol blue powder (Fisher Scientific # MBX-14107)
    0.25 g of xylene cyanol (Fisher Scientific # AC-42269-0250)
    Add: 1 mL 1 M Tris (pH 8)

Live/Prepared Materials

- Order the pUC19 (plasmid) DNA (New England BioLabs # N3041S or N3041L) and lambda DNA (New England BioLabs # N3011S or N3011L) from New England BioLabs or another biological supply house.

- Lambda DNA molecular weight marker and pUC19 DNA can be stored at –20°C indefinitely. The enzymes are shipped overnight on dry ice. They are stable for months as long as they are stored at –20°C in a freezer that is *not* self-defrosting. The enzymes should not be moved for more than a few minutes from this temperature and then should always be kept on ice. Depending on the skill level of your students, you may choose to add the DNA and enzymes to their microtubes personally at the appropriate time in the lab procedure. Have students bring their tubes to your desk.

Reference Materials

Micklos, D. A., and G. A. Freyer. 2003. *DNA Science,* 2nd ed. Cold Spring Harbor, NY: Cold Spring Harbor Laboratory Press.

Sambrook, J., and D. W. Russell. 2012. *Molecular Cloning: A Lab Manual,* 4th ed. Cold Spring Harbor, NY: Cold Spring Harbor Laboratory Press.

Checklist of Materials

Equipment

For each four students

gel electrophoresis apparatus:
_____ gel holder (1)
_____ comb (1)
_____ chamber for electrophoresis (1)
_____ chamber cover (1)
_____ power supply with electrodes (1 set)
_____ staining tray (1)
_____ lab bench liner taped to bench under electrophoresis set up and prep area (optional)
_____ micropipettors and tips or microcapillary pipettes and plunger; various sizes from 1–100 µl (many)
_____ thermometer (1)
_____ metric ruler (1)
_____ agarose
_____ holding rack or tray for microtubes (1)
_____ permanent marker (1)
_____ practice gel in petri dish
_____ empty microtubes
_____ beaker with colored glycerine water

Demonstration/Supplies Table

Equipment

For each class

_____ microcentrifuge (optional) (1)
_____ 37°C incubator or water bath (1)
_____ 55°C incubator or water bath (1)
_____ digital camera (1)
_____ light box (to view gels)

_____ Nalgene™ Labtop Cooler
_____ Blue light transilluminator
_____ disposable gloves (1 box)
_____ waste disposal bag

Solutions/Chemicals

For each four students

_____ 1× TAE for gel chamber (or alternate TBE buffer)
Color-coded microtubes at student work area:
_____   DI water and *Ava* II buffer (A) (1)
_____   DI water and *Pvu* II buffer (P) (1)
_____   DI water and *Ava* II buffer for double digest (AP) (1)
_____   gel loading dye (1)
_____   DI water (for loading dye #1) (1)
_____   DI water (for uncut DNA #6) (1)
Color-coded microtubes in cold box:
_____   DI water and lambda DNA molecular weight markers (1)
_____   DI water and lambda DNA low molecular weight markers (optional #7)

For each class

_____ supply of pUC19 DNA
_____ supply of *Ava* II restriction enzyme
_____ supply of *Pvu* II restriction enzyme (optional)
_____ methylene blue solution
_____ agarose solutions with SYBR® Safe added (no stain added if using methylene blue)

LAB TOPIC 11

Population Genetics I: The Hardy-Weinberg Theorem

After completing several labs with intensive preparations, this lab will be a welcome relief! Use the free time to clear a path through the preparation room! Although the lab manual suggests that students may work in groups of three or four, we strongly suggest that they work in groups of two. This ensures that all students participate.

In our laboratory program, we begin this lab by performing a simple exercise with PTC paper (Carolina Biological Supply # 174010) and control paper (Carolina Biological Supply # 174000). Using this exercise immediately engages students in the concepts to be studied. Pass out a piece of each type of paper to every student and have him or her place on their tongues first the control and then the PTC paper. Then count the number of tasters and nontasters in the class and calculate class frequencies for each phenotype. Point out that among Americans of European descent, about 70% are tasters (can taste the chemical PTC—phenylthiocarbamide) and 30% are nontasters (cannot taste the chemical). Compare these statistics with the frequency of tasters and nontasters in your class. Write on the board the number of tasters, the percent tasters, and the frequency of tasters. Do the same for nontasters. Then use these numbers to determine the allelic frequencies by taking the square root of the frequency of nontasters. Use this activity as a basis for your introductory discussion. It would be interesting to separate the students into different ethnic groups for this experiment, if you have adequate numbers. For comparison of frequencies refer to "Global Variation in Sensitivity to Bitter-Tasting Substances (PTC or PROP)" at https://www.nidcd.nih.gov/health/statistics/global-variation-sensitivity-bitter-tasting-substances-ptc-or-prop.

For Each Two Students

- brown paper lunch bag

  Although small plastic bags may be used, we prefer to use brown paper bags so students cannot see the color of the beads and sampling will be completely random. Reuse the same bags for several labs, but check the condition of the bags daily and replace worn or torn bags when needed.

- beads of two colors in plastic cups

  Most experiments call for 100 beads initially, 50 each of two colors; however, frequencies of alleles (beads) change with successive generations, and the migration experiment calls for 100 beads of each color. For these reasons, we suggest that each pair of students begins with approximately 200 beads, 100 of each color. Alternatively, have extra supplies of each color at each student work area. We use the pop beads that we used for Lab Topic 7 Mitosis and Meiosis (Carolina Biological Supply # 171100).

  You may also purchase beads from a craft store. Pop beads work better than perfectly round beads because they do not roll as far when students drop them on the floor!

- additional copies of Table 11.5.

  Students will need additional copies of this table, depending on how many scenarios they investigate. They must have one table per scenario. This table can be down-loaded from www.masteringbiology.com. Students select Study Area, Lab Media, Investigating Biology Lab Data Tables—9th edition. Instructors select Instructor Resources. On the Instructor Home page, choose Instructor Guides for Supplements, and then Data Tables from Investigating Biology Lab Manual, 9e.

For Each Four Students

- computers with Tables 11.3, 11.4, and 11.5 downloaded in Excel format from www.masteringbiology.com (see pathway above). Students can record their data and analyze the results.

Exercise 11.3

- computer software

  There are several suitable programs, including:

  (1) *Evolve* in the BioQUEST Library:
      http://bioquest.org/BQLibrary/library_result.php
      Scroll down the list to find Evolve.

  (2) Simulation software and resources for population biology:
      http://www.cbs.umn.edu/populus/

  (3) PopG Genetic Simulation Program. Version 4.02. 2015. Requires Java. Download program:
      http://evolution.gs.washington.edu/popgen/popg.html

  (4) Red Lynx: Population Genetics Simulator. Web based program with graphs and data output:
      http://scit.us/redlynx/

- computer hardware

  Two or three students may work together at one computer.

  If students are to use a computer lab to complete the simulations, make arrangements for the use of the facility, download the programs, or provide the links to simulations. If the instructor demonstrates the program in lab, then only one computer will be needed. Most computer labs also have projectors available for classroom instruction. BioQUEST software is PC and Mac compatible.

Instructor's Desk

- projection technology (computer with digital projector or document camera, or overhead projector)
- Tables 11.3, 11.4, and 11.5 downloaded in Excel format from www.masteringbiology.com in Instructor Resources. Students can record their data and analyze the results.
- USB drive

Checklist of Materials

Equipment

For each student (if performing taster/non-taster introductory activity)

_____ PTC paper
_____ control paper

For each two students

_____ brown paper lunch bag
_____ plastic cups containing 200 beads, 100 each of two colors
_____ additional beads as needed
_____ computer software
_____ extra copies of Table 11.5

For each four students

_____ computer with Tables 11.3, 11.4, and 11.5 downloaded in Excel format from www.masteringbiology.com. Web access or simulation program downloaded.

Instructor's Desk

_____ projection technology (computer with digital projector or document camera, or overhead projector)
_____ Tables 11.3, 11.4, and 11.5 downloaded in Excel format from www.masteringbiology.com
_____ USB drive

LAB TOPIC 12

Bacteriology

Students work individually or in pairs on most activities, but they are asked to share observations among several pairs for the milk succession experiment (Exercise 12.2) and bacteria in the environment (Exercise 12.3).

If you have oil immersion objectives available on your microscopes, demonstrate their use to your students. We do not have these objectives on microscopes used in our introductory biology labs, and this has not been an impediment to the lab.

If you have other bacterial cultures on hand in your lab, you may choose to substitute them for the bacterial cultures suggested in this preparation. Any nonpathogenic bacterial species that will grow on nutrient agar can be substituted.

One note about safety: Students should seal all plates that they prepare, and they should not open them for their observations. We remind students to do this in each laboratory exercise.

For Each Student

- stereoscopic microscope, Exercise 12.1, Lab Study A
- compound microscope
- microscope slides (We have students supply their own.)
- prepared slide of bacterial types, Exercise 12.1, Lab Study B (Carolina Biological Supply # 293964)

  Alternatively, have one example of each of the three types of bacteria on demonstration microscopes.

- 15-cm metric ruler

For Each Two Students

- 4 sterile nutrient agar plates, Exercises 12.3, 12.4
- wax pencil
- Parafilm strips to seal plates

Exercise 12.1, Lab Study B; Exercise 12.2

- dropper bottle of DI water
- squirt bottle of DI water
- dropper bottle of crystal violet stain
- clean toothpicks
- clothespin
- timer or clock with second hand
- discard container containing a weak bleach solution, labeled for used tooth picks

84

Exercise 12.1, Lab Study C; Exercise 12.2

- dropper bottles of:
  DI water
  crystal violet stain
  Gram iodine (same recipe as I_2KI used in previous labs)
  safranin
  95% ethyl alcohol/acetone
- squirt bottle of DI water

Exercise 12.3, Experiments A and B; Exercise 12.4

- 2 cotton-tipped sterile swabs (Fisher Scientific # 14-959-92B) in a capped test tube
- sterile water in a capped test tube
- bacterial inoculating loop

For Each Four Students

- hand soap (bar or liquid antibacterial soap for hand washing)

Exercise 12.1, Lab Studies A and B

- spray bottle of disinfectant (dilute household bleach, 70% ethyl or isopropyl alcohol)
- alcohol lamp with matches
- disposal container (a 500-mL beaker or large finger bowl, labeled)
- staining tray or pan

Exercise 12.1, Lab Study C; Exercise 12.4, Lab Study A

- bacterial broth cultures, containing a wooden, cotton-tipped swab:
  Micrococcus luteus
  Bacillus megaterium
  Serratia sp.
  E. coli

Demonstration/Supplies Table

- 24-in. $\times$ 30-in. autoclavable biohazardous waste disposal bag (Fisher Scientific # 01-826, available in various sizes, e.g. # 01-826-6 is 24-in. $\times$ 30-in.)
- extra disinfectant for cleaning up a spill
- box of disposable gloves

Exercise 12.1, Lab Study A

- 6 different species of bacteria growing on agar plates

  Use 100 mm $\times$ 15 mm petri dishes throughout this lab study (Fisher Scientific # 08-757-12). We suggest you use bacteria *Bacillus megaterium, Bacillus subtilis* var. *niger, E. coli, Serratia* sp., *Micrococcus luteus, Micrococcus roseus, Sarcina* sp. (see notes about growing these bacteria), or use species of your choice. In a class of 24 students, we have 4 of each of the 6 species. This means that each student will have a plate to examine. Students can then swap plates until they examine a total of three plates. Tape the plates closed and they can be used all week.

Exercise 12.1, Lab Study C

- broth cultures or plates (2 each) of *Micrococcus, Bacillus, Serratia,* and *E. coli* inoculated within 24 hours of the lab for best results with Gram stain

  If these cultures are older, they may become gram-variable. We prefer to use broth cultures for this lab study.

Exercise 12.2

- pH paper, 0–14 range, 0.5 sensitivity (Carolina Biological Supply # 893930)
- TGY (tryptone, glucose, yeast) agar plates of each of the aged milk types

  Have 2 of each of the 6 different aged milk plates per laboratory (a total of 12 plates): 2 of each 8-day plain and chocolate, 4-day plain and chocolate, and 1-day plain and chocolate. Two students will work with one plate. The pair should first observe the plate with the unaided eye and determine if there are bacteria only, bacteria and fungi, or fungi only. They should then make slides of all different bacteria on the plate. If there appears to be only one bacterial species on the plate, both students should make a slide of the one species present. We do not plate the milk that has been continuously refrigerated, but you may choose to do this. Bacteria do not grow on these plates.

- 100-mL beaker or flask of each of the milk types

  Have 2 beakers of each of the aged milk treatments on the demonstration table (a total of 12 beakers). In addition, have 1 beaker with continuously refrigerated chocolate milk and 1 beaker with continuously refrigerated plain milk. Students may check the pH and texture of milk in the refrigerated milk beakers to compare with the aged milk. Students take the aged milk beaker that corresponds to their plate culture to their work area, make observations, and return the beaker to the demonstration table.

  Each student pair should then exchange observations with others in the class until Table 12.3 is completely filled in.

Exercise 12.3

- piece of raw chicken in a petri dish (for Team 1)
- soil sample in a petri dish (for Team 2)
- pond water sample in a small vial or petri dish (for Team 4)
- some plant part: leaf, flower part, and so on (for Team 5)
- bar of hand soap for the experiment (for Team 6)

Exercise 12.4

- antibiotic disk dispenser, loaded with disk magazines (for example, Carolina Biological Supply # 806605)
- blank disks soaking in disinfectants
- blank disks soaking in antiseptics
- blank disks soaking in DI water
- forceps in alcohol

For week 2, when students observe the results of their experiments, place large labels on the demonstration table and have students place their cultures in the appropriate area for all students to observe and record results.

Instructor's Desk

- projection technology (computer with digital projector or document camera, or overhead projector)
- photomicroscopy system (optional)

Greenhouse or Field Supplies

For plant parts (Exercise 12.3—Team 5), just before lab, collect leaves, flowers, or other plant structures from plants in the greenhouse or around the campus.

Grocery Supplies

The following should be purchased from the grocery store: chicken, antiseptics (various kinds: rubbing alcohol, Listerine™, hydrogen peroxide, and so forth), disinfectants (various kinds: Clorox™, Lysol™, ammonia, and so forth), soap (antibacterial for general washing and bar soap for the experiment), plain and chocolate whole milk.

Equipment: Staining Trays

Staining trays may be purchased from Carolina Biological Supply (# 742001). These are quite expensive, and you will need one for each group of four students. We made our own using 9-in. × 5-in. bread loaf baking pans. We purchased strong wire and cut it into lengths slightly longer than the length of the pan, two for each pan. Then we drilled two holes about 1–2 inches below the rim in each end of each pan, making sure the holes were at the same level. Then we inserted the wires through the holes, making sure each wire was level. For safety, we sanded down the ends of the wires or covered them with tape.

Solution Preparation Notes

Crystal Violet

1. Add 2 g crystal violet (Carolina Biological Supply # 856150) to 20 mL of 95% ethanol.
2. When the crystal violet dissolves, add 80 mL of 1% solution of ammonium oxalate (Carolina Biological Supply # 844166).
3. Mix well and filter before use.

Gram Iodine (I2KI)

1. To make 100 mL, dissolve 2 g potassium iodine (KI) (Carolina Biological Supply # 883789) in 100 mL DI water.
2. Add 1 g iodine (I_2) (Carolina Biological Supply # 868982) and stir until dissolved.

This stain is light sensitive. Store in a dark bottle away from light.

0.5% Safranin Solution

Dissolve 0.5 g safranin (Carolina Biological Supply # 887039) in 100 mL DI water.

Ethyl Alcohol/Acetone

Add 1 part 95% ethyl alcohol to 1 part acetone to make this 1:1 mixture.

Nutrient Agar Plates

Use 100 mm × 15 mm sterile petri dishes (Fisher Scientific # 08-757-12).

Purchase dehydrated nutrient agar (not plain agar) from any biological supply house (Carolina Biological Supply # 785301) and follow the directions on the container for making plates. A typical recipe follows:

1. In a 2-L flask, mix 23 g nutrient agar in 1 L of DI water until evenly dispersed.
2. Heat using constant stirring until dissolved.
3. Cover with a loose cotton plug or foam stopper covered loosely with foil.
4. Autoclave* at 15 psi for 15 minutes.
5. Allow to cool slightly (you should be able to hold the flask with your bare hands) and pour just enough agar to cover the bottom into sterile petri dishes.
6. Invert plates and refrigerate after completely cooled.

One liter makes about 40 plates.

Nutrient Broth

Purchase nutrient broth from any biological supply house (Carolina Biological Supply # 785361) and follow the directions on the container. A typical recipe follows:

1. In a 2-L flask, dissolve 8 g in 1 L of DI water until evenly dispersed.
2. Cover with a loose cotton plug or foam stopper covered with foil. The foil should not be tight.
3. Autoclave at 15 psi for 15 minutes.
4. Allow the broth to cool before inoculating with bacteria.

TGY (Tryptone, Glucose, Yeast Extract) Agar Plates

To culture the bacteria in milk, use TGY plates.

1. Add 10 g tryptone (Carolina Biological Supply # 216741), 1 g glucose (Sigma-Aldrich # G 8270), 5 g yeast extract (Sigma-Aldrich # Y 0875), and 15 g agar (not nutrient agar) (Carolina Biological Supply # 842133; Fisher Scientific # BP1423-500) to 1 L of DI water in a 2-L flask.
2. Mix until evenly dispersed.
3. Heat using constant stirring for several minutes.
4. Autoclave at 15 psi for 15 minutes.
5. Pour solution into petri dishes (just enough to cover the bottom of the dish). Let plates sit until agar solidifies.
6. Invert plates and refrigerate until needed.

One liter makes about 40 plates.

Disinfectants/Antiseptics

Try any variety of disinfectants: Clorox (3–8% sodium hypochlorite solution), Lysol, ammonia, vinegar, other cleaning products; and any variety of antiseptics: rubbing alcohol, hydrogen peroxide, Listerine, bactericidal soaps, baking soda.

Using a hole punch on index cards, make disks to float in the disinfectants/antiseptics.

Antibiotics and Dispenser

Bacterius LTD (www.bacteria.us.com) is a company that sells Difco and BBL microbiology products. The company offers 6-place and 8-place antibiotic disc dispensers and

---

*If you do not have an autoclave, you can boil all liquids for 15 minutes to sterilize. Watch constantly, as agar and broth solutions scorch easily. Remove from heat, cool slightly, and pour. Glassware can be sterilized in an oven, 121°C (250°F) for 30 minutes.

susceptibility test disc cartridges on its website. The dispenser is expensive, but it can be used indefinitely, and it is extremely efficient when dispensing multiple discs in the laboratory. Carolina Biological Supply offers a kit (# 154740) with six antibiotic disk magazines and other supplies for antibiotic sensitivity testing. Also available is a single Sensi-Disc® Dispenser (Carolina Biological Supply # 806601). MSS MedSuppliesShop sells a Sensi-Disc Dispenser BBL (#260459) at a more reasonable price.

Antibiotics and dispensers are available through other distributors as well, for example, Fisher Scientific (see Appendix).

Order a variety of antibiotics such as ampicillin, bacitracin, erythromycin, kanamycin, novobiocin, penicillin, streptomycin, and tetracycline. Search "antibiotic disks" on Carolina Biological and Fisher Scientific websites.

Disinfectant for Cleaning Tabletops and Spills

Use the disinfectant to clean up spills and to wipe down tabletops before and after the lab activities.

Although a 20% solution of household bleach works better, we prefer 70% EtOH or 70% isopropyl alcohol (rubbing alcohol) because bleach will ruin clothes. If you use household bleach, dilute it 1:5. Dispense to each set of four students in spray bottles and keep the extra on the demonstration table.

Live/Prepared Materials

Order the following bacterial agar tube or plate cultures from a biological supply house to arrive about 10 days before the first lab:

- *Bacillus megaterium* (Carolina Biological Supply# 154900)
- *Escherichia coli* (Carolina Biological Supply # 155065)
- *Serratia marcescens* (Carolina Biological Supply # 155450)
- *Sarcina lutea* (Carolina Biological Supply # 155420)
- *Micrococcus luteus* (Carolina Biological Supply # 155155), and *Micrococcus roseus* (Carolina Biological Supply # 155160)

Carolina Biological also has a pigmented bacteria set (# 154745) that includes *Micrococcus luteus* (yellow), *Rhodococcus rhodochrous* (pink), *Sarcina aurantiaca* (orange-yellow), and *Serratia marcescens* (red). Prepare plate cultures for Exercise 12.1, Lab Study A, and broth cultures for Exercise 12.1, Lab Study C, and Exercise 12.4, Lab Study A. Ask microbiologists in your department for suggestions of additional species.

We often have difficulty growing *Sarcina*. *Bacillus subtilis* var. *niger* will be black if grown on a special media containing tyrosine. We sometimes use *Bacillus cereus* (Carolina Biological Supply # 154870), which grows in beautiful swirls but often contaminates other cultures. *M. roseus* plates must grow about 5 days before they appear rosy. All of the bacteria suggested will grow on nutrient agar.

The following information may be useful:

Type	Optimum Temperature (°C)	Description
Escherichia coli	25–37	gram (–) rods
Bacillus subtilis	25–30	gram (+) motile rods
Bacillus megaterium	30	gram (+) large rods
Bacillus cereus	30	gram (+) motile rods
Micrococcus luteus	25	gram (+) cocci in clusters yellow pigment
Micrococcus roseus (appears only after about 4 days)	25	gram (–) motile rods rose pigment
Serratia marcescens	25	gram (–) motile rods red pigment
Sarcina lutea (appears only after about 4 days)	25	gram (+) cocci yellow pigment
Rhodococcus rhodochrous	25	gram (+) rods rose pigment
Sarcina aurantiaca	25	gram (+) cocci orange pigment
Aquaspirillum itersonii	30	gram (–) motile spirals

Bacterial Stock Cultures

Make a stock culture of each bacterial species according to the following directions:

1. Add about 300 mL of nutrient broth to each of six 500-mL flasks.
2. Sterilize in an autoclave or steam sterilizer according to the directions for the sterilizer.
3. Allow the broth to cool.
4. Using a sterile cotton-tipped applicator, swab the purchased bacterial culture tube to load the applicator with bacteria.
5. Swirl the loaded applicator in the 300 mL of sterile nutrient broth.
6. Incubate culture at appropriate temperature until needed.

Bacterial Plate Cultures

At least 2 days before lab, inoculate nutrient agar plates according to the following directions:

1. Load a sterile cotton-tipped applicator with bacteria by inserting it into the stock culture.
2. Using the loaded applicator, swab the top third of the plate to make a lawn.
3. Using a flamed loop, draw one wavy streak of bacteria out of the lawn to isolate individual bacteria for the colony morphology study (Exercise 12.1, Lab Study A).
4. Invert plates and incubate at the correct temperature until lab.

You can prepare these plates earlier and refrigerate them after you see good bacterial growth. If you intend to use plates rather than broth cultures for the Gram stain, *Bacillus* and *Micrococcus* should be plated no earlier than 24 hours before lab to obtain correct Gram stain results. After 24 hours these cultures will become gram-variable.

Bacterial Broth Cultures in Test Tubes

1. About 2 days before lab, dispense nutrient broth into as many test tubes as needed.
2. Add one wooden, cotton-tipped swab and color-coded caps to identify the bacterial species.
3. Autoclave and cool the broth tubes.
4. Inoculate the tubes with the appropriate bacteria by taking the swab from the tube, dipping it into the stock culture, and replacing it into the broth tube.
5. Store inoculated broth tubes at appropriate temperatures until needed. Do not store the innoculated cultures more than 2–3 days as the broth and bacteria will be absorbed by the wooden swab handle and should not be touched by students. If you have labs throughout the week, prepare multiple sets at 2-day intervals.

You will prepare 2 sets of broth cultures of the bacteria *Bacillus*, *Serratia*, *E. coli*, and *Micrococcus*. The first set is used for the Gram stain (Exercise 12.1, Lab Study C) and must be inoculated less than 24 hours before the lab. We usually do this in the afternoon for the next day's lab. Have 2 cultures of each for each lab (a total of 8 cultures). The second set is used by students to make the lawns for Exercise 12.4, Lab Studies A and B. Make one set of the 4 bacteria for each four students (a total of 6 cultures of each for every class of 24, for a total of 24 cultures). This means that you will need 32 broth cultures per lab.

Aging and Plating Milk (Exercise 12.2)

1. About 10 days before lab, pour fresh chocolate and white milk into separate 100-mL beakers labeled "24-hour chocolate," "4-day chocolate," "8-day chocolate," "24-hour white," "4-day white," and "8-day white." Make enough for two of each type of milk per lab.
2. Cover with foil.
3. Allow the milk to sit at room temperature for the prescribed time, then refrigerate to arrest bacterial and fungal growth.
4. Use the aged milk in these beakers to make the plates and for student observations during lab. The beakers may be reused if you keep them refrigerated up to the time of lab and return them to the refrigerator immediately after lab.
5. The day of lab, pour 1 beaker of chocolate milk and 1 beaker of white milk that has been continually refrigerated. Students should measure the pH and describe this for comparison.

About 2–3 days before lab:

1. Plate each type of aged milk on a separate TGY plate. Use a sterile Pasteur pipette or a sterile swab to place several drops of milk culture or a generous swab at one edge of a sterile TGY plate. Apply both liquid and solid portions of the milk.
2. Use a flamed and cooled Bacti-Spreader (or a sterile swab) to spread the milk over about one-third of the plate to make a lawn.
3. Use a flamed loop to pull out a wavy streak of bacteria from this lawn.
4. Repeat with each type of milk.
5. Incubate plates at room temperature until needed.

Be sure to use fresh, sterile applicators each time you change to a new milk. Make enough plates for two of each type of milk per lab and a fresh set of plates for each lab.

Cleanup

Autoclave all used plates and other disposable waste—everything that has come into contact with bacteria—in autoclavable disposal bags (see Fisher Scientific numbers above; Carolina Biological Supply # 647055). (Be sure to have a large pan under the bags, as they usually leak. We double-bag everything.) Dispose of all disposable items in the trash. After autoclaving, dispose of all solid agar in the trash, not the sink. If agar is still liquid, allow it to cool and solidify before disposing of it in the trash. Autoclave all test tubes and cultures. After autoclaving, the broth can be poured down the drain.

Checklist of Materials

Equipment

For each student

_____ compound microscope (1)
_____ stereoscopic microscope (1)
_____ microscope slides (several)
_____ metric ruler (1)
_____ prepared slide of three bacterial types (or have this on demonstration)

For each two students

_____ sterile water in capped test tube (1)
_____ bacterial inoculating loop (1)
_____ clothespin (1)
_____ timer or clock with second hand
_____ discard container with a weak bleach solution, labeled for used toothpicks

For each four students

_____ clean toothpicks (4)
_____ wax pencils (2)
_____ cotton-tipped sterile swabs (4) (2 each in 2 capped test tubes)
_____ alcohol lamp and matches (1)
_____ disposal container (1)
_____ hand soap (1 bar or container of antibacterial soap)
_____ bar of soap for experiment
_____ staining rack or tray (1)

Greenhouse or Field Supplies

_____ various plant structures

Grocery Supplies

_____ chicken
_____ disinfectants
_____ antiseptics
_____ soaps

Live/Prepared Materials

For each student

_____ prepared slide: bacterial types (1 for each student, or see Demonstration/ Supplies Table, following)

For each two students

_____ sterile nutrient agar plates (4)

For each class

6 different species of bacteria on agar plates (4 of each species). Choose from:
_____ *Micrococcus luteus* (4)
_____ *Micrococcus roseus* (4)
_____ *Sarcina sp.* (4)
_____ *Serratia sp.* (4)
_____ *E. coli* (4)
_____ *Bacillus megaterium* (4)
_____ *Bacillus subtilis* (4)

bacterial nutrient broth cultures (2 of each species less than 24 hours old for Gram stain, 6 of each species for lawns):
_____ *Micrococcus* (8)
_____ *Bacillus* (8)
_____ *Serratia* (8)
_____ *E. coli* (8)

Demonstration/Supplies Table

For each class

_____ demonstration of bacterial cell types on compound microscopes (1 bacillus, 1 coccus, 1 spirillum—only if each student does not have a slide)
_____ autoclavable biohazardous waste disposal bag (1)
_____ piece of raw chicken in petri dish (1)
_____ soil sample in petri dish (1)
_____ pond water sample in small vial (1)
_____ leaf or other plant part

100-mL beakers of plain whole milk (2 sets of 3 aged types plus 1 beaker of constantly refrigerated; all may be reused):
_____ constantly refrigerated (1)
_____ 1 day old (2)
_____ 4 days old (2)
_____ 8 days old (2)

100-mL beakers of chocolate milk (2 sets of 3 aged types plus 1 beaker of constantly refrigerated; all may be reused):
_____ constantly refrigerated (1)
_____ 1 day old (2)
_____ 4 days old (2)
_____ 8 days old (2)
_____ TGY agar plates (2 sets of each aged milk type, total of 12; may not be reused)

_____ antibiotic disk dispenser, loaded with disks (1)
_____ blank disks soaking in disinfectants (1 of each type)
_____ blank disks soaking in antiseptics (1 of each type)
_____ blank disks soaking in DI water (1 container)
_____ forceps in alcohol (several pairs in 1 container)
_____ extra disinfectant for cleaning up a spill
_____ disposable gloves (1 box)

Instructor's Desk

For each class

_____ projection technology (computer with digital projector or document camera, or overhead projector)
_____ photomicroscopy system (optional)

Solutions/Chemicals

For each two students

_____ squirt bottle of DI water (1)
dropper bottles:
_____   DI water (1)
_____   crystal violet (1)
_____   Gram iodine (1)
_____   safranin (1)
_____   ethyl alcohol/acetone (1)
_____   sterile nutrient agar plates (4)

For each four students

_____ disinfectant in spray bottle (1)

For each class

_____ pH paper (1 box)

Protists

The debate about classification of the protists continues. The organization of this lab topic reflects classification for this group as presented in the latest editions of most introductory biology texts. The following table, similar to Table 13.1 in the lab manual, is included here to summarize the examples and the sequence of investigations. Students work independently as they view prepared microscope slides, prepare slides of living organisms, and review demonstrations; however, throughout these activities, they should discuss their observations with their research partners and be prepared to propose an investigation of protists to be performed in Exercise 13.5. It is important that from the beginning of the laboratory students begin to consider possible questions to investigate as they observe the organisms. See Exercise 13.5, pages 362-363 in the laboratory manual for a list of potential questions.

Clades and Examples of Protists Investigated in Lab Topic 13

Supergroup	Clade	Lab study	Examples
Excavata (Exercise 13.1)	Euglenozoans	13.1A	Kinetoplastids—*Trypanosoma*
		13.1B	Euglenids—*Euglena* sp.
"SAR" (Exercise 13.2)	Stramenopiles	13.2A	Diatoms Brown algae Water mold—*Saprolegnia*
	Alveolates	13.2B	Ciliates—Paramecia Dinoflagellates Apicomplexan—*Plasmodium sp.*
	Rhizarians	13.2C	Foraminiferans Radiolarians
Unikonta (Exercise 13.3)	Amoebozoans	13.3A	Tubulinids—*Amoeba* sp.
		13.3B	Plasmodial slime molds—*Physarum* Cellular slime molds—*Dictyostelium*
Archaeplastida (Exercise 13.4)	Red algae	13.4A	Rhodophytes—*Porphyra*
	Green algae	13.4B	Chlorophytes—*Spirogyra,Ulva, Chlamydomonas,* Charophytes—*Chara*

New in this edition, we have included a template that can be used to assist student teams in developing their proposals. Using a template will simplify evaluating their proposals and preparing the materials needed for their open-inquiry investigations.

For Each Student

- compound microscope
- stereoscopic microscope
- slides and coverslips
- dropper bottles of water
- forceps

Exercise 13.1

- prepared slides of:
    - *Trypanosoma* sp. (Carolina Biological Supply # 295798) (Lab Study A)
    - *Euglena* sp. (Carolina Biological Supply # 295666) (Lab Study B)

Exercise 13.2

- prepared slides of
    - diatomaceous earth. (Carolina Biological Supply # 295972—online only) (Lab Study A). The laboratory exercise calls for students to study living diatoms and then view a prepared slide of diatomaceous earth on demonstration. You may choose to modify this and have a slide of diatomaceous earth for each student in addition to the living cultures.
    - *Saprolegnia* w.m. (Carolina Biological Supply # 297508) (Lab Study A)
    - Dinoflagellates (if living organisms are not available) (Carolina Biological Supply # 295306) (Lab Study B)
    - *Plasmodium* sp. (Carolina Biological Supply # 297190 – in human blood) (Lab Study B)
    - Foraminiferans (Carolina Biological Supply # 296870) (Lab Study C)

Exercise 13.4, Lab Study B

- prepared slides of
    - *Chlamydomonas* sp. (Carolina Biological Supply # 296398)
    - *Spirogyra* sp. (Carolina Biological Supply # 296548 and # 296554; Triarch #-2-30bb and 2-30cc)

For Each Four Students

- Protoslo or other quieting agent
- dropper bottle of 1% acetic acid (Exercise 13.2, Lab Study B)
- dropper bottle of yeast stained with Congo red (Exercise 13.2, Lab Study B)

Exercise 13.1, Lab Study B

- living culture of *Euglena* sp. (Carolina Biological Supply # 151351) with a transfer pipette

> For all the living cultures mentioned in this lab prep, one living culture for each four students is ideal. If you have only one or two cultures of living organisms per lab room, place these on the Demonstration/Supplies table with transfer pipettes. Warn students not to mix the pipettes.

Exercise 13.2

- living cultures, each with a transfer pipette
  - diatoms (Carolina Biological Supply # 151287 – a field-collected mixed culture. Single species cultures are also available. Try the pinnate forms *Navicula* (#153045) and *Synedra* (#153095) (Lab Study A)
  - *Paramecium caudata* (Carolina Biological Supply # 131554) (Lab Study B)
  - *Paramecium caudata* fed yeast stained with Congo red (optional – instructor adds yeast stained with Congo red to one culture 1-2 hours before lab) (Lab Study B)
  - dinoflagellates (Carolina Biological Supply # 131750) (Lab Study B)

Exercise 13.3, Lab Study A

- living cultures of *Amoeba proteus* (Carolina Biological Supply # 131306)

Exercise 13.4, Lab Study B

- living cultures of *Chlamydomonas* sp. (Carolina Biological Supply # 152030)
- living cultures of *Spirogyra* sp. (Carolina Biological Supply # 152525)
- living or preserved *Chara* sp. (Carolina Biological Supply # 162120)

Demonstration/Supplies Table

Place a card with identifying information beside each item on demonstration.
- diatomaceous earth slide on a compound microscope (Carolina Biological Supply # 295972) (Exercise 13.2, Lab Study A)
- examples of brown algae (Phaeophyta) (Exercise 13.2, Lab Study A)
- agar plate cultures of *Saprolegnia* with forceps and dropper bottles of water (have several plates available, depending on your class size) (Carolina Biological Supply # 156271) (Exercise 13.2, Lab Study A)
- radiolarian skeletons slide on a compound microscope (Carolina Biological Supply # 296840) (Exercise 13.2, Lab Study C)
- *Physarum* growing in a petri dish (have several dishes available, depending on your class size) (Carolina Biological Supply # 156193) (Exercise 13.3, Lab Study B)
- *Dictyostelium* growing in a petri dish (have several dishes available, depending on your class size) (Carolina Biological Supply # 155996) (Exercise 13.3, Lab Study B)
- examples of red algae (Rhodophyta) (Exercise 13.4, Lab Study A). You can purchase nori in Asian food markets.
- preserved or living specimen of *Ulva lactuca* (sea lettuce) (Marine Biological Laboratory # 2140 – call for pricing; available throughout the year). Sea lettuce is also available for human consumption. Try Maine Coast Sea Vegetables online (www.seaveg.com). (Exercise 13.4, Lab Study B)
- living or preserved specimen of *Chara* sp. (Carolina Biological Supply # 162121) (Exercise 13.4, Lab Study B)

- Carolina Biological Supply offers online a variety of living seaweed that has been collected fresh and shipped from Maine. Examples are the brown algae *Ascophyllum* (# 151405), *Fucus* (# 151415), and *Laminaria* (#151420); the red algae *Chondrus* (#151410) and *Porphyra* (# 1151425); and the green algae *Ulva* (# 151430).

If you have only one or two containers for each of the living cultures listed under **For Each Four Students**, place these cultures on the supplies table with an identifying label and a transfer pipette in each. You may need to spread these out to avoid congestion at the table.

Exercise 13.5, Designing and Performing an Open-Inquiry Investigation

Have sufficient amounts of all the supplies on the Demonstration Table available for students to use for their investigations.

If your campus has a convenient pond or other body of water, you might allow students to survey the pond and describe the diversity of protists as their investigation. In this case, you should have available sampling equipment such as plankton nets, jars, labels, and equipment to take samples from the bottom.

Bulletin Board Display

- wall charts diagramming the life cycle of *Plasmodium* sp. (Exercise 13.2, Lab Study B)

Instructor's Desk

- projection technology (computer with digital projector or document camera, or overhead projector)
- photomicroscopy system (optional)
- Many images of the life cycle of the malaria parasite are available online. If computers are available, choose one of these to project and review for students.

Grocery, Greenhouse, and Nursery Supplies

- yeast (to feed Paramecium – Exercise 13.2, Lab Study B)
- supplies for Exercise 13.5 Designing and Performing an Open-Inquiry Investigation
  - oat flakes, sugar, aluminum foil
  - aquarium mold retardant from pet store
  - *Chrysanthemum* and *Yucca* plants
  - commercial chemicals that may control water mold

Additional Supplies for Exercise 13.5

- buffers for different pHs
- small lamps

Solution Preparation Notes

1% Acetic Acid

Add 10 mL acetic acid to 990 mL DI water. Dispense in dropper bottles.

Yeast Stained with Congo Red

1. Add one package (¼ oz) baking yeast to 100 mL DI water. Stir until dissolved.
2. Add 0.2 g Congo red pigment (Carolina Biological Supply # 855348). Stir until dissolved.

Students will add the stained yeast cells to the edge of the coverslip covering their *Paramecium* slide. They should watch as the yeast diffuses around the *Paramecium* to observe the intake of the yeast cells.

Nutrient Agar Plates

To prepare agar plates for Exercise 13.5 (Student Designed Investigation), use nutrient agar (Carolina Biological Supply # 785301).

1. Mix 23 g nutrient agar in 1 L of DI water until evenly dispersed.
2. Heat using constant stirring until dissolved.
3. Cover with a loose cotton plug or foam stopper covered loosely with foil.
4. Autoclave at 15 psi for 15 minutes.
5. Allow to cool slightly (you should be able to hold the flask with your bare hands) and pour just enough agar to cover the bottom into sterile petri dishes.
6. Invert plates and refrigerate after completely cooled.

For students' experiments, vary the recipe by substituting 1% glucose or sucrose, 1% albumin, or 6, 7, or 8 pH buffers for the DI water. You may also make some plates with oat flakes added to the medium or moistened with 1–2 drops of sterile water and dropped on top after the plates have solidified.

Live/Prepared Materials

Growing *Physarum*

1. Prepare petri dishes with agar (not nutrient agar). Suspend 20 g of agar in 1 L of DI water.
2. Heat while stirring to dissolve agar, and autoclave at 15 psi for 15 minutes.
3. Allow to cool slightly and pour plates. After the plates have cooled, sprinkle the agar with a few oatmeal flakes. Moisten the oatmeal with 1–2 drops of sterile water.
4. Use sterile forceps to add a piece of filter paper with *Physarum* sclerotium (Carolina Biological Supply # 156190, 156193) to the agar-oatmeal plate.
5. Wet the filter paper with a drop of sterile water. Place in the dark.
6. After 24–48 hours, use sterile technique to transfer squares of agar with pieces of the active plasmodium to additional petri dishes with agar and oatmeal. Place the agar block plasmodium-side down.
7. Keep cultures in the dark.
8. Transfer cultures every 3–4 days if kept at room temperature, or cultures may be refrigerated and kept for long periods of time.

Reference Materials

If it is possible to have fresh or preserved plankton samples available in the laboratory, the following reference materials may be useful to help identify organisms:

An invertebrate biology text
A botany text

A protozoa identification book
An algae identification book, for example:

Prescott, G. W., J. Bamrick, and E. Cawley, 1978, 3rd edition. *How To Know the Fresh Water Algae.* Columbus: McGraw-Hill Science.

Other useful references:

Needham, James G., and Paul R. Needham. 1962. *A Guide to the Study of Fresh-Water Biology.* New York: McGraw-Hill.

Palmer, C. Mervin. 1962. *Algae in Water Supplies.* Public Health Service Publication No. 657. U.S. Dept. of Health, Education and Welfare, Public Health Service. Washington, D.C.

Smith, D. S. 2001 *Pennak's Freshwater Invertebrates of the United States: Porifera to Crustacea,* 4th edition. New York: Wiley.

Checklist of Materials

Equipment

For each student

_____ compound microscope (1)
_____ stereoscopic microscope (1)
_____ slides (several)
_____ coverslips (several)

For each four students

_____ dropper bottle of DI water (1)
_____ dropper bottle of 1% acetic acid (1)
_____ Protoslo (1 bottle)
_____ dropper bottle of yeast stained with Congo red (1)

Live/Prepared Materials

For each student

prepared slides of:
_____ *Trypanosoma* sp (1)
_____ *Euglena* sp (1)
_____ diatomaceous earth (1) (if living cultures are not available)
_____ *Saprolegnia* (1)
_____ dinoflagellates (1) (if living cultures are not available)
_____ *Plasmodium* sp. (1)
_____ foraminiferans (1)
_____ *Chlamydomonas* sp.(1)
_____ *Spirogyra* sp. (1)

Demonstration/Supplies Table

For each class

Living or preserved cultures, each with a transfer pipette

_____ diatoms

_____ *Paramecium caudata*

_____ *Paramecium caudata* fed yeast stained with Congo red (optional)

_____ dinoflagellates

_____ *Chlamydomonas* sp.

_____ *Amoeba proteus*

_____ *Spirogyra* sp.

_____ *Chara*

Microscope slides on a compound microscope

_____ diatomaceous earth

_____ radiolarian skeletons

Demonstration materials of macroscopic algae:

_____ Examples of brown algae (Phaeophyta)

_____ Examples of red algae (Rhodophyta)

_____ Preserved or living *Ulva lactuca* (Chlorophyta)

_____ Preserved or living *Chara* sp. (Charophyta)

Cultures growing in petri dishes

_____ *Saprolegnia* with forceps and water dropper bottles

_____ *Physarum*

_____ *Dictyostelium*

Supplies for students' investigations

Instructor's Desk and Bulletin Board

_____ projection technology (computer with digital projector or document camera, or overhead projector)

_____ photomicroscopy system (optional)

_____ life cycle of *Plasmodium* wall charts or downloaded images

Protists Research Proposal

Team Name: **Team Members:**

Date: **Instructor:**

Question:

Hypothesis:

Prediction:

Summary of the Procedures:

Describe briefly the steps of your procedures, paying attention to the organisms, solutions, containers, equipment and instrumentation that will be required. Consider the number of replicates, environmental conditions, and variables to be measured. As you develop your procedure, you may want to design a table for collecting data and copy to a USB drive to download on the computers in lab.

Materials:

List the materials that are required to implement your research. Include the organisms, glassware, solutions, tools, and equipment or instruments that you will need for your experiments. Include the numbers for each and other details that may be important.

Plant Diversity I: Bryophytes (Nonvascular Plants) and Seedless Vascular Plants

Students should work independently on slides and in pairs for all other work. We place one complete set of slides for this lab topic and Lab Topic 15 in a numbered small plastic slide box at the appropriate student work area. This reduces breakage and allows you to track missing slides. Organize the demonstration materials to follow the order of the lab. Prepare cards to indicate the lab study and exercise as well as the taxon.

We recommend that you use living moss, liverwort, horsetails, whisk ferns, and fern materials whenever possible. Keeping with the latest classification schemes, note that we include whisk ferns (*Psilotum*) and horsetails with ferns in the phylum Monilophyta (Exercise 14.2, Lab Study B).

Laboratory instructors may find it helpful to have a photomicroscopy system available to assist students in locating structures on their microscope slides. Take care, however, that students do not rely on projected images rather than observing their own slides.

For Each Student
- compound microscope
- 2 dissecting needles

Exercise 14.1, Lab Study A
- prepared slides of:
    moss antheridia l.s. (Carolina Biological Supply # 298992)
    moss archegonia l.s. (Carolina Biological Supply # 299028)
- colored pencils

Exercise 14.2, Lab Study A
- prepared slide of *Selaginella* strobilus l.s. showing microspores and megaspores (Carolina Biological Supply # 299878)
- living *Selaginella* with megasporangia in leaf axils (Carolina Biological Supply # 157016)

Exercise 14.2, Lab Study C
- slides
- coverslips
- stereoscopic microscope (can be shared by students)
- prepared slides of:
    fern gametophyte w.m. with archegonia (Carolina Biological Supply # 299272)
    fern gametophyte with young sporophyte w.m. (Carolina Biological Supply # 299356)

For Each Four Students

- dropper bottle of DI water
- dropper bottle of glycerol (concentrated; slightly diluted works also)

Demonstration/Supplies Table

Exercise 14.1

Ask the instructor if students will also bring in their own examples.

- living moss cultures (gametophyte and sporophyte generations) (Carolina Biological Supply # 156695 and 156730), Lab Study A
- living liverwort (gemmae cups with gemmae) (Carolina Biological Supply # 156540) Lab Study B. Carolina Biological Supply # 223001 is a preserved set of four stages in the life cycle of liverworts, including gemmae cups with gemmae. Contact Carolina about purchasing only the preserved gemmae cup stage.

Exercise 14.2

If possible, provide more than one example of these plants. We include several different ferns and fern allies in our collection.

- living *Selaginella* (Carolina Biological Supply # 157016—spikes with megasporangia in leaf axils, and 157010—living *Selaginella* called resurrection plant), Lab Study A
- living *Lycopodium* (Carolina Biological Supply # 156980 and 156990), Lab Study A
- living and/or preserved whisk fern, *Psilotum* Lab Study B. Check local nurseries and/or college greenhouses for available specimens. Also available to order from Black Jungle Exotics www.blackjungleterrariumsupply.com/Psilotum_nudum_p_1894.html.
- living and/or preserved horsetails, *Equisetum* (with strobili) (available in a kit of fern allies, Carolina Biological Supply # 156950), Lab Study B. Also check local nurseries. Horsetails are popular plants to grow in residential ponds.
- living fern sporophytes (with sori) (Carolina Biological Supply # 156902), Lab Study C
- living fern gametophytes (prothalli) with archegonia and antheridia (Carolina Biological Supply # 156879), Lab Study C. Have Protoslo available to use with fern sperm. If a video-microscopy system is available, use this to show fern sperm to the entire class.
- living fern gametophytes with young sporophytes attached (Carolina Biological Supply # 156881), Lab Study C

Exercise 14.2, Lab Study D

- fossils of extinct lycopods: *Lepidodendron* and *Sigillaria*
- fossils of extinct sphenopsids: *Calamites*
- fossils of extinct ferns: *Alethopteris*

All of these fossils are available at Geological Enterprises. See notes below and the Appendix for contact information.

Instructor's Desk

- projection technology (computer with digital projector or document camera, or overhead projector)
- photomicroscopy system (optional)

Greenhouse Supplies

The instructor may ask students to bring in examples of mosses or ferns. In many areas, examples of these (and perhaps horsetails) can be collected locally.

Mosses, ferns, lycopods, and horsetails may be available at nurseries or local greenhouses. Although the prep calls for only one example of each, we try to include a variety of examples whenever possible. Biological supply houses will have living and preserved plant material. The living plants in this exercise are easy to grow and maintain in the greenhouse or terraria. We have been successful dividing established plants rather than ordering new sets. The best specimens (particularly for whisk ferns) are often provided by botanical gardens, college and university greenhouses, or nursery greenhouses in the area.

Live/Prepared Materials

Living plants can be ordered from biological suppliers if they are not available in the greenhouse or locally.

Fern Gametophytes

Fern gametophytes can be ordered but are easy to grow. Students can start their own earlier in the semester by sprinkling spores on peat pellets that are kept moist or by using the Fern Minimarsh kits available from Carolina Biological Supply (# 156820).

Fossil Plants

Fossil specimens are available from biological suppliers, but they may also be available from geologists at your institution. Our students enjoy seeing fossils collected from our region.

The fossils listed in Exercise 14.2 are available at Geological Enterprises. Also, you might check rock and gem shows in your area, as they are often another good source for fossils. Ward's no longer sells plant fossils with the exception of fern fossils (*Alethopteris*, Wards # 535720) and Calamites fossils (Wards # 535750). We have also located fern fossils for sale using an online search.

C-Fern™ Kits for Investigative Extensions

- Chemical Attraction: C-Fern™ Sperm Chemotaxis kit (contact Carolina Biological Supply for availability; # 156702 is a kit that allows students to see swimming sperm)
- Meet the C-Fern™ kit (Carolina Biological Supply # 156700)

    Web address for C-Fern: http://www.c-fern.org/. Also see the ABLE C-fern activity (Chapter 10, Vol. 19, 1998) and additional information on Carolina Biological website.

Checklist of Materials

Equipment

For each student

_____ compound microscope (1)
_____ stereoscopic microscope (1)
_____ slides (several)

_____ coverslips (several)
_____ 2 dissecting needles
_____ colored pencils (1 set)

For each four students

_____ dropper bottle of DI water (1)
_____ dropper bottle of glycerol

Live/Prepared Materials

For each student

prepared slides of:
_____   moss antheridia l.s. (1)
_____   moss archegonia l.s. (1)
_____   fern gametophyte w.m. (1) (provide if living gametophytes are not available)
_____   fern gametophyte with young sporophyte w.m. (1) (provide if living materials are not available)
_____   *Selaginella* strobilus l.s. (1)
_____   preserved *Selaginella* (1) (students may share)

Demonstration/Supplies Table

For each class

living:
_____   moss (1 set)
_____   liverworts (1 set of examples) (use preserved if living are not available)
_____   *Selaginella* (1 example)
_____   *Psilotum* (1 example)
_____   *Lycopodium* (1 example)
_____   horsetails (1 example)
_____   ferns (1 set of examples)
_____   fern gametophytes (or preserved) (1 culture)
fossils of extinct:
_____   lycopods (1)
_____   sphenopsids (1)
_____   ferns (1)
_____ Protoslo

Instructor's Desk

_____ projection technology (computer with digital projector or document camera, or overhead projector)
_____ photomicroscopy system (optional)

For Investigative Extensions

_____ C-Fern kits

Plant Diversity II: Seed Plants

Students should work independently on slides and in pairs for all other work. We place one complete set of slides for this lab topic and Lab Topic 14 in a numbered small plastic slide box at the appropriate student work area. This reduces breakage and allows you to track missing slides. Organize the demonstration materials to follow the order of the lab. Prepare cards to indicate the lab study and exercise as well as the taxon.

If a photomicroscopy system is available, you may use this to help students find structures on their slides. Take care, however, that students do not rely on projected images rather than observing their own slides.

For Each Student

- compound microscope
- stereoscopic microscope
- slides
- coverslips
- dropper bottle of DI water

Exercise 15.1, Lab Study B

- prepared slides of:
    male staminate cones l.s. (Carolina Biological Supply # 301436)
    female ovulate cones l.s. (Carolina Biological Supply # 301460)
    pine pollen (Carolina Biological Supply # 301448) (if students do not make their own pine pollen slides)
- colored pencils

Exercise 15.2, Lab Study C

- dropper bottle of pollen tube growth medium
- petri dish with filter paper to fit inside
- dissecting probe
- brush bristles, sand, or glass chips
- prepared slides of:
    lily anthers (Carolina Biological Supply # 304586)
    lily ovary (Carolina Biological Supply # 304694)

For Each Two Students

Exercise 15.2, Lab Study A

- living flowers to dissect (We recommend gladiolus and three other species.)
- stereoscopic microscope
- wax pencil

Demonstration/Supplies Table

Exercise 15.1, Lab Study A

- living or pressed examples of conifers, ginkgo, cycads, and Mormon tea (*Ephedra*). Check your local herbarium for specimens of these plants. Also, nursery supply houses usually have ginkgo and cycads, called sago palm (*Cycas*) or cardboard palm (*Zamia*), for sale. If you have a greenhouse or if it is possible on the grounds of your college, you could begin your own living collection by planting specimens. Mormon tea (*Ephedra nevadensis* or *E. viridis*) can be purchased as seeds from some online herbal medicine websites.

Exercise 15.1, Lab Study B

- living or preserved pine branch with female cones and male cones
- preserved pine pollen
- prepared slide of pollen grains (pine pollen: Carolina Biological Supply # 301448) (mixed angiosperm pollen: Carolina Biological Supply # 304264)

  Have these slides on demonstration if students do not make their own slides.

  Carolina Biological Supply offers a preserved set of Pine Life Cycle for 25 students that includes male and female cones, seed, seedling, and twig with needles. (Carolina Biological Supply # 223316)

Exercise 15.2, Lab Study B

A variety of flowers selected to fit the key. Have these flowers identified or numbered on the demonstration table. Students must key each flower.

Exercise 15.2, Lab Study C

- flowers for pollen germination
- set of prepared slides showing stages of ovule development. Use for demonstration or review. (Carolina Biological Supply # 304628, # 304634, # 304640, # 304646, # 304652, # 304670, # 304694) (Triarch microscope slides of ovule development #s 19-0 to 19-12)
- Check for images of the lily life cycle including ovule and stamen development at: ny.wisc.edu/Resources/Botany/Angiosperms/Lilium%20Life%20Cycle/.

Exercise 15.2, Lab Study D

Variety of fruits and seeds to show all types of fruits and different methods of seed dispersal. We number each fruit on the demonstration table and require that students key each fruit to determine its type (e.g., drupe).

Instructor's Desk

- projection technology (computer with digital projector or document camera, or overhead projector)
- photomicroscopy system (optional)

Greenhouse Supplies

Living Plants/Flowers/Pollen

Living examples of the gymnosperms are far superior to pressed and preserved specimens. Why not plant ginkgos and cycads on campus, if they are hardy in your region? Contact a local plant nursery for suggestions. We prepare our own preserved collections of pine cones in the spring of the year. We place 1-, 2-, and 3-year-old cones together in a tall jar for use in other seasons.

Make friends with your local florist, greenhouse, and nursery managers! Some will provide slightly past-their-peak flowers for use in the laboratory. Our farmers' market also stocks large quantities of cut flowers at reasonable rates. Look for flowers with characteristics that can be used with the pollination key. We keep a carrion or starfish plant in our greenhouse for the fly-pollinated flower (sometimes it even flowers for lab). Ask your florist for suggestions based on the characteristics for each pollinator type. Avoid flowers with large numbers of petals; their other reproductive structures are usually poorly formed.

Check for pollen germination from a variety of flowering plants available in the greenhouse or in the wild. At the suggestion of Rodney Scott of Wheaton College, we keep bridal veil (a popular plant that blooms all year and is used in hanging baskets) in the greenhouse. Several students may share one flower and obtain pollen by touching the anthers of the intact flower to the drop of pollen tube growth medium on the slide. Pollen from yellow or white sweet clover (*Melilotus officinalis* or *Melilotus alba*) also readily germinates. These plants are common "weeds" along roadsides in the spring and early summer in some regions. Pollen from petunia and kudzu usually germinates easily. Other suggested plants for pollen germination include: spiderwort, snapdragon, lilies, sweetpeas, and *Brassica rapa* (fast plants).

Grocery Supplies

Fruits

The instructor may ask students to bring examples of fruits to lab. Examples are limited only by your local grocer or farmers' market. Suggestions include:

achene—sunflower "seeds," dandelion
nut—acorns, hickory nuts, walnuts, pecans (these should include the husk and seed)
capsule—okra (dried)
follicle—milkweed (dried), magnolia
legume—pea pods, green beans, peanuts
drupe—olive, peach, plum, cherry
berry—tomato, green pepper, orange, squash, watermelon
pome—pear, apple
multiple fruit—pineapple, fig
aggregate fruit—strawberry (achenes are the hard "seeds"), blackberry

Provide the laboratory instructor with a list of the fruit types selected for lab. Do not label fruits by type, since students are expected to determine the type using the key in the lab manual. If you are not sure of the type of fruit, these are usually described in taxonomic keys (*Manual of Cultivated Plants* by L. H. Bailey, Macmillan Publishing Co., 1949). Fruit types and examples can also be found at Wayne's Word (http://waynesword.palomar .edu/fruitid1.htm). Cut the fruits in half (cross section) so that students can determine the location and number of seeds for fleshy fruits.

Solution Preparation Notes

Pollen Tube Growth Medium

1. Measure out:

   100 g sucrose

   0.1 g H_3BO_3

   0.3 g $Ca(NO_3)_2 \cdot 4\,H_2O$

2. Add DI water up to 1000 mL.

We have successfully germinated a few species of pollen in a simple 10% or 20% sucrose solution. The growth medium is more reliable, however. You also might try varying the sucrose concentration in the growth medium, adding twice the amount or half the amount.

FAA (formalin, alcohol, acetic acid)

FAA is a good, all-purpose fixative for plant materials. If you find plant materials in the field that can be used in this lab topic (for example, male and first and second year female pine cones), collect them and preserve them in jars with this fixative.

To make 100 mL:

   95% Ethanol - 50 mL

   glacial acetic acid - 5 mL

   formalin (37% formaldehyde) - 10 mL

   DI water - 35 mL

Live/Prepared Materials

Living plants and flowers may be available in the greenhouse, from local suppliers, at farmers' markets, nurseries, or growing outside.

Brush Bristles

Purchase children's paintbrushes. Trim off the bristles and dispense into petri dishes. You could also use a few sand grains or glass chips to prevent crushing the pollen.

Checklist of Materials

Equipment

For each student

_____ compound microscope (1)

For each two students

_____ stereoscopic microscope
_____ slides (several)

_____ coverslips (several)
_____ colored pencils (2 different colors)
_____ dissecting probe (2)
_____ brush bristles in petri dish (1)
_____ petri dish with filter paper inside (1)
_____ flowers to dissect

Live/Prepared Materials

For each student

prepared slides of:
_____ male staminate pine cones l.s. (1)
_____ female ovulate pine cones l.s. (1)
_____ pine pollen
_____ lily anthers (1)
_____ lily ovary (1)

Demonstration/Supplies Table

For each class

_____ living or pressed examples of conifers, ginkgos, cycads, and Mormon tea (1 of each)
_____ living or preserved pine branch with female cones (1-, 2-, and 3-year-old cones) and male cones (several)
_____ preserved pine pollen (1 container)
_____ variety of fruits and seeds (1 of each)
_____ prepared slide of pollen grains (1) (optional)
_____ slides showing ovule development in a flower bud

Instructor's Desk

_____ projection technology (computer with digital projector or document camera, or overhead projector)
_____ photomicroscopy system (optional)

Greenhouse Supplies

For each class

_____ living flowers for flower anatomy (many)
_____ living flowers for pollination study (many)
_____ living flowers for pollen (several)

Solutions/Chemicals

For each two students

dropper bottles of:
_____ pollen growth medium (1)
_____ DI water (1)

Bioinformatics: Molecular Phylogeny of Plants

In Lab Topic 16 students address questions about the evolutionary history of plants, using their knowledge of morphology and life cycles from previous lab experiences (Lab Topics 14 and 15, Plant Diversity I and II). After posing hypotheses, they utilize the tools of bioinformatics to analyze nucleotide sequences of the rubisco gene for a diverse group of algae and plants. Students will access the National Center for Biotechnology Information (NCBI) using the Web interface Biology WorkBench. The images for the nine plant species are now inserted in the margin of the lab topic as well as being available at the Mastering Biology website. Check for connectivity to the website and run the sequence analysis prior to scheduling this lab topic. The laboratory is designed for students to complete the analysis and to prepare a report during the laboratory period.

Nucleotide sequences for the algae and plants are available at www.masteringbiology.com in the Study Area under Lab Media and then select *Investigating Biology* Lab Material. Download the files, keeping the images in one folder named "Images" and the nucleotide sequences in a second folder named "rbcL nucleotide seq." These two folders can then be copied to the desktop for each student computer.

For Each Two Students

- a computer with Web access
- 2 computer desktop folders: "images" and "rbcL nucleotide seq"
- printer access
- 24 sheets of 11" × 17" plain white paper
- scissors and cellophane tape

Demonstration/Supplies Table

Optional living examples include *Chara, Polytrichum, Marchantia, Equisetum, Polypodium, Pinus, Zamia, Arabidopsis,* and *Lilium.* Check the plants you used in Lab Topics 14 and 15 for possible examples to be used in Lab Topic 16.

Instructor's Desk

- projection technology (computer with digital projector or document camera, or overhead projector)

Reference Materials (Web Resources)

Biology WorkBench home page:
http://workbench.sdsc.edu

DNA Subway, educational resources for teaching and open inquiry investigations:
http://www.iplantcollaborative.org/learning-center/dna-subway

National Center for Biotechnology Information home page and information on rooted and unrooted phylogenies:
http://www.ncbi.nlm.nih.gov/
http://www.ncbi.nlm.nih.gov/Class/NAWBIS/Modules/Phylogenetics/phylo9.html

University of California Berkley, understanding evolution website with excellent pages of phylogenetics:
http://evolution.berkley.edu/evolibrary/home.php

Checklist of Materials

Equipment

For each two students

_____ computer with Web access
_____ computer desktop folders: "images" and "rbcL nucleotide seq"
_____ sheets of 11" × 17" plain white paper (24)
_____ scissors and cellophane tape

For each class

_____ printer access
_____ Web resources

Instructor's Desk

_____ projection technology (computer with digital projector or document camera, or overhead projector)
_____ USB drive

The Kingdom Fungi

This lab topic was added to the sequence of labs in *Investigating Biology* in the eighth edition to follow the sequence of chapters in most introductory biology textbooks, and to reflect molecular evidence that shows a close relationship of the fungi and animal kingdoms. In the 9th edition we have modified several figures and added a new figure illustrating the life cycle of the ascomycete *Peziza*, one of the organisms studied in this lab topic. We provide extensive coverage of the major groups of fungi, including lichens. In addition, we have added new suggestions for open-inquiry investigations that can be performed in Exercise 17.2.

New in this edition, we have included a template that can be used to assist student teams in developing their proposals. Using a template will simplify evaluating their proposals and preparing the materials needed for their open-inquiry investigations.

This is a lab where we encourage students to collect organisms from nature to bring to lab. However, be sure to warn students not to eat any fungi that they collect. For many species, only experienced mycologists can distinguish between edible and poisonous mushrooms. Students may collect from wooded areas on campus or in nearby parks. Encourage them to explore fallen trees or woodpiles. Students might even be lucky enough to see a fairy-ring of mushroom basidiocarps in the campus lawn. You can use their collections for demonstrations or students may use them in an open-inquiry investigation.

For Each Student

- compound microscope
- stereoscopic microscope
- slides and coverslips
- dissecting needles

Exercise 17.1, Lab Study A

- prepared slide of *Rhizopus* with sporangia and zygosporangia (Carolina Biological Supply # 297782)

Exercise 17.1, Lab Study B

- prepared slide of *Peziza* ascocarp (Carolina Biological Supply # 297980)
- prepared slide of *Penicillium* (Carolina Biological Supply # 297968)

Exercise 17.1, Lab Study C

- prepared slide of *Coprinus* pileus sections (Carolina Biological Supply # 298176)

- fresh mushroom basidiocarp purchased in a grocery store. Try to purchase those where the pileus, stipe, and gills are present and visible.
- mushrooms collected from nature (optional – but this adds more interest to the lab exercise, especially if you allow students to make a spore print)

Exercise 17.1, Lab Study D

- prepared slide of sections through lichens (Carolina Biological Supply # 298476)
- fresh lichens to allow students to make a wet mount to observe hyphae and photo-synthetic cells

For Each Two Students

Exercise 17.1, Lab Study A

- ethyl alcohol in a small beaker
- forceps
- alcohol lamp and matches
- dropper bottle of DI water
- *Rhizopus* culture (on the Demonstration Table—students take one to their lab station to study)

Demonstration/Supplies Table

Prepare a card describing each demonstration and/or supply, naming the appropriate laboratory exercise. Place demonstrations on the table in the order studied in the lab manual.

Exercise 17.1, Lab Study A

- petri dish cultures of *Rhizopus stolonifer* with sporangia (Carolina Biological Supply # 156223). Optimally, have one plate per pair of students. Several days before lab, use a flamed spatula to add wedges of agar and *Rhizopus* cut from a commercially prepared plate to sterile nutrient agar plates to create as many plates of organisms as needed.
- cultures of *Pilobolus crystallinus* (Carolina Biological Supply # 156207) growing on rabbit dung agar, displayed on a stereoscopic microscope

Exercise 17.1, Lab Study B

- demonstration materials of dried or preserved *Peziza* (Ward's Science # 630065)
- cultures of *Penicillium* in petri dishes (Carolina Biological Supply # 156146) and collections of green mold growing on fruits/foods in your refrigerator, or you might see some in your grocery
- demonstration materials of Roquefort or blue cheese from the grocery store
- demonstration materials of fresh, preserved, or dried morels (*Morchella*). The most popular biological supply houses no longer carry preserved morels. However, dried edible morels can be purchased from several sites on the Web. Try: eBay and Walmart (Hoosier Hill Farm). Also try farmer's or specialty markets in your area.
- ergot ascocarps in rye or wheat. The plastic mounts formerly offered by Carolina Biological Supply are no longer available. It is relatively easy to find ergot in wild grasses and in bags of organic rye grain, however. Microscope slides of ergot are available from Triarch #s 3-20A – 3-20C and Carolina Biological Supply # 297908. You might call biological suppliers to check for availability of examples of ergot.

Exercise 17.1, Lab Study C

- fresh or preserved examples of club fungi: bird's nest fungi, puffballs, shelf fungi, and corn smut.
- Have on demonstration a can of corn smut, also called corn mushroom (cuitlacoche or huitlacoche) available to order online at MexGrocer.com.

Exercise 17.1, Lab Study D

- examples of crustose, foliose, and fruticose lichens

Collect these from wooded areas. To add interest, ask your students to collect these to bring to lab. Use fresh lichens to allow students to make wet mounts to observe hyphae and photosynthetic cells. Carolina Biological Supply offers a living set of different types of lichens: # 156400.

Exercise 17.2

The following is a beginning list of supplies to have available for students' independent investigations. If students have special requests, try to have available the materials they request. Make an overhead transparency or write on the board all supplies available for students to use with their investigations.

- cultures of *Pilobolus crystallinus, Rhizopus, Penicillium*
- sterile agar plates to grow each species
- sterile agar plates with sugar (see directions below)
- sterile agar plates with albumin
- sterile agar plates prepared with buffers pH 6, 7, or 8
- sterile potato dextrose agar plates
- aluminum foil
- small lamp
- various breads from the health food store: wheat, rye, corn, potato, rice
- bread with and without preservatives
- sterilized dung from various animals
- cultures of living bacteria, e.g., *E. coli*
- filter paper disks to use with fungal or lichen extracts
- mycorrhizae inoculate (An online search for myhcorrhizae will yield several sources where mycorrhizae may be purchased, for example, Skunk Labs Endo Mycorrhizae Powder and Granular Endo Mycorrhizae.)
- sterile forest soil (microwave samples to kill bacteria and fungi)
- natural forest soil

Instructor's Desk

- projection technology (computer with digital projector or document camera, or overhead projector)
- photomicroscopy system (optional)

Grocery Supplies

- mushrooms
- Roquefort and/or blue cheese
- bread with and without preservative (for students' experiments)
- various breads from the health food store

- check in stores, farmers markets, or produce vendors that sell organic produce for fresh corn with corn smut infections. Feel the ear of corn through the husks, and if you feel large lumps, check for smut infection.
- cans of corn mushroom (cuitlacoche or huitlacoche)

Solution Preparation Notes

Nutrient Agar Plates

To prepare agar plates for Exercise 17.2, use nutrient agar (Carolina Biological Supply # 785301).

1. Mix 23 g nutrient agar in 1 L of DI water until evenly dispersed.
2. Heat using constant stirring until dissolved.
3. Cover with a loose cotton plug or foam stopper covered loosely with foil.
4. Autoclave at 15 psi for 15 minutes.
5. Allow to cool slightly (you should be able to hold the flask with your bare hands) and pour just enough agar to cover the bottom into sterile petri dishes.
6. Invert plates and refrigerate after completely cooled.

For students' experiments, vary the recipe by substituting 1% glucose or sucrose,1% albumin, or 6, 7, or 8 pH buffers for the DI water.

Checklist of Materials

Equipment

For each student

_____ compound microscope (1)
_____ stereoscopic microscope (1)
_____ blank slides (several)
_____ coverslips (several)
_____ dissecting needles (2)

For each two students

_____ ethyl alcohol in a small beaker
_____ forceps
_____ alcohol lamp with matches
_____ dropper bottle of DI water

Live/Prepared Materials

For each student

prepared slides of:
_____ *Peziza* ascocarp l.s. (1)
_____ *Coprinus* c.s. (1)
_____ living mushroom (1)

For each two students

_____ living *Rhizopus* culture (1) (on the Demonstration Table—students take one to their lab station to study)

Demonstration/Supplies Table

For each class

_____ *Pilobolus* growing on rabbit dung agar
_____ dried or preserved *Peziza*
_____ preserved or fresh morels
_____ plastic mounts of ergot in rye or wheat, or preserved examples
_____ *Penicillium* cultures
_____ Roquefort or blue cheese
_____ can of corn mushroom (cuitlacoche or huitlacoche)
_____ examples of crustose, foliose, and fruticose lichens
_____ supplies for students' investigations

Instructor's Desk

_____ projection technology (computer with digital projector or document camera, or overhead projector)
_____ photomicroscopy system (optional)

Fungi Research Proposal

Team Name: Team Members:

Date: Instructor:

Question:

Hypothesis:

Prediction:

Summary of the Procedures:

Describe briefly the steps of your procedures, paying attention to the organisms, solutions, containers, equipment and instrumentation that will be required. Consider the number of replicates, environmental conditions, and variables to be measured. As you develop your procedure, you may want to design a table for collecting data and copy to a USB drive to download on the computers in lab.

Materials:

List the materials that are required to implement your research. Include the organisms, glassware, solutions, tools, and equipment or instruments that you will need for your experiments. Indicate if you are collecting fungi or lichens from the field or will need assistance. Include the numbers for each and other details that may be important.

Animal Diversity I: Porifera, Cnidaria, Platyhelminthes, Mollusca, and Annelida

Students should work independently on all slides and dissections. However, since preserved *Nereis* worms are expensive, if your budget is limited you might have students work in pairs on *Nereis* and the earthworm dissections. Students do not dissect the preserved sponges, so they can be used for many labs. We place the preserved sponges in small containers at students' individual work areas. All other living and preserved animals are placed on the demonstration/supplies table. In our labs, each student's work area is numbered, and we place one complete set of slides in a correspondingly numbered small plastic slide box at the appropriate work area. This allows us to track missing slides and reduces breakage.

Laboratory instructors may find it helpful to have a photomicroscopy system with digital projection available to assist students in locating and orienting structures as they study microscopic slides. Take care, however, that students do not rely on projected images rather than observing their own slides. In addition to improving microscope skills, searching a slide and observing variations in slides are valuable exercises.

We do not provide gloves for students. They are asked to purchase a personal supply.

We continue to study the invertebrates in the sequence that reflects the latest evidence in animal phylogeny. Keep in mind, however, that the study of animal systematics is a work in progress and conclusions about evolutionary relationships among animals may change as new molecular evidence emerges.

For Each Student

- watch glass or petri dish
- stereoscopic microscope
- compound microscope
- disposable gloves

    We ask students to supply their own. If you provide them for students, choose from the selection of gloves at VWR Scientific # 32916, or from the selection beginning at Carolina Biological Supply # 706337.

- dissecting instruments (2 dissecting needles, good quality scissors, blunt probe, forceps, scalpel)

    We ask students to purchase a personal dissecting kit that contains each of these items and a small metric ruler.

- dissecting pan
- dissecting pins
- hand lens (optional)

Exercise 18.1

- preserved sponge, *Scypha* or *Grantia* (Carolina Biological Supply # 224005; Connecticut Valley Biological # P4)
- prepared slide of *Scypha* or *Grantia* l.s. (Carolina Biological Supply # 305842)

Exercise 18.2

- depression slide
- microscope slides and coverslips
- living *Hydra* (Carolina Biological Supply # 132800)
- living water fleas, *Daphnia* (Carolina Biological Supply # 142314)
- pipettes and bulb
- prepared slide *Hydra* c.s. and l.s. (Carolina Biological Supply # 306118) or l.s. only (Carolina Biological Supply # 306052)

Exercise 18.3

- living planarian, *Dugesia* (Carolina Biological Supply # 132950)
- pieces of liver
- prepared slides of *Dugesia:*

  w.m. (Carolina Biological Supply # 306318), digestive system colored

  c.s. (Carolina Biological Supply # 306330), planaria composite. Three different regions are presented.

Exercise 18.4

- preserved clam or freshwater mussel (Carolina Biological Supply # 224844)

  If fresh clams are available in your local farmers' market or grocery store, you might have one of these dissected as a demonstration or substitute fresh clams for preserved clams.

Exercise 18.5, Lab Study A

- preserved clamworm, *Nereis*, large (Carolina Biological Supply # 225045; Ward's #68v2302; Connecticut Valley Biological # P116). If supplies are limited, have two students work together on *Nereis* and the earthworm. One student can dissect one, the partner the other. Each may then demonstrate the dissection to the other.

Exercise 18.5, Lab Study B

- preserved earthworm, *Lumbricus,* large (Carolina Biological Supply # 225012; Ward's # 68v2202; Connecticut Valley Biological # P110)
- alternatively or in addition to preserved earthworms, living earthworms (Carolina Biological Supply # 141620, or check with local bait shops)
- prepared slide of *Lumbricus* c.s. (Carolina Biological Supply # 307246)

For Each Four Students

- dropper bottle of water
- dropper bottle of 1% acetic acid
- dropper bottle of methylene blue

Demonstration/Supplies Table

- various examples showing the diversity of complex sponges
- all cultures of living organisms

- preserved animals, 1 per student
- stock supply of liver (Keep frozen and dispense small pieces as needed.)

Alice Lindahl, Department of Biology, Utah State University, suggests using *Cordylophora lacurstris* in place of *Hydra*. *Cordylophora* is a colonial, brackish-water hydroid with many advantages over *Hydra*. Parent colonies may be obtained from Woods Hole Oceanographic Institute, and cultures may be maintained indefinitely in small jars. Keep them in dim light, and use droppers to feed newly hatched brine shrimp to polyps every couple of days. To expand colonies or to prepare specimens for student use, add a drop of ⅛-strength seawater to a microscope slide. Use sewing thread to firmly tie a piece of the parent colony to the slide. Submerge the slide in dilute seawater in a small jar. Students may observe and feed the organisms directly in the culture jar.

Instructor's Desk

- projection technology (computer with digital projector or document camera, or overhead projector)
- photomicroscopy system (optional)

Maintaining Living Organisms

- *Daphnia* or small *Artemia* (to feed *Hydra*)

  Maintain at cool room temperature or at 15°C. If cultures are large enough, supply mild aeration. *Artemia* need aeration in particular.

- *Planaria* and *Hydra*

  Maintain at cool, constant room temperature or at 15°C.

Solution Preparation Notes

1% Acetic Acid

Add 10 mL acetic acid (Carolina Biological Supply # 841290) to 990 mL DI water.

0.1% Methylene Blue

Dissolve 1 g methylene blue powder (Carolina Biological Supply # 875684) in 1000 mL DI water.

Checklist of Materials

Equipment

For each student

_____ compound microscope (1)
_____ dissecting microscope (1)
_____ hand lens (optional) (1)
_____ watch glasses or petri dishes (2)
_____ depression slides (2)
_____ Pasteur pipettes with bulbs (4)
_____ dissecting pan (1)

_____ dissecting instruments (1 set)
_____ dissecting pins (1 set)
_____ disposable gloves (if provided) (1–2 pairs)

Live/Prepared Materials

For each student

live:
_____ *Hydra* (1)
_____ *Daphnia* (2–3)
_____ *Dugesia* (1)
_____ liver for *Dugesia*
preserved:
_____ *Scypha* or *Grantia* (1)
_____ *Nereis* (1)
_____ *Lumbricus* (1)
_____ mussel (or clam) (1) (or substitute fresh specimen)
prepared slides of:
_____ *Scypha* or *Grantia* l.s. (1)
_____ *Hydra* c.s. and l.s. or c.s. only (1)
_____ *Dugesia* w.m. and c.s. (1 each)
_____ *Lumbricus* c.s. (1)

Demonstrations

_____ diversity of complex sponges
_____ stock supply of liver

Instructor's Desk

_____ projection technology (computer with digital projector or document camera, or overhead projector)
_____ photomicroscopy system (optional)

Solutions/Chemicals

For each four students

_____ dropper bottle of water (1)
_____ dropper bottle of 1% acetic acid (1)
_____ dropper bottle of methylene blue (1) (optional)

Animal Diversity II: Nematoda, Arthropoda, Echinodermata, Chordata

Students work independently on all dissections and slides. Since the fetal pig is observed only superficially, two students can share one for this lab, although in the Vertebrate Anatomy labs to follow, each student should have his or her own pig to dissect. Add the slides to the slide box with those studied in Animal Diversity I. This means that all slides for both labs will be available for students to review after all dissections and observations are completed.

For Each Student

- dissecting pan
- dissecting instruments (2 dissecting needles, scissors, blunt probe, forceps, scalpel)

    We have students supply their own dissecting tools.

- disposable gloves

    We ask students to supply their own. If you provide them for students, choose from the selection of gloves at VWR Scientific # 32916, or from the selection beginning at Carolina Biological Supply # 706337.

- hand lens (optional)

Exercise 19.1

- preserved *Ascaris* (Ward's # 680802, Carolina Biological Supply # 224405)

    These usually arrive with only a few males. Separate male and female worms and distribute these so students may see each sex dissected. You may choose to place a dissected male worm on demonstration with parts labeled.

- prepared slide of *Ascaris* c.s. male and female (Carolina Biological Supply # 306918)

Exercise 19.2, Lab Study A

- preserved crayfish

    We purchase both plain (not injected) and single-injected crayfish in equal numbers. The injection process destroys the heart but demonstrates blood vessels well. The heart is more easily seen in plain specimens. Pass out crayfish so that each pair of students will have one plain and one injected crayfish (plain: Carolina Biological Supply # 225300, Connecticut Valley Biological # P1840; injected: Carolina Biological Supply # 225310, Connecticut Valley Biological # P1850).

Exercise 19.2, Lab Study B

- preserved grasshopper *Romalea* (Carolina Biological Supply # 225580)

Exercise 19.3

- preserved sea star (Carolina Biological Supply # 226011)

Exercise 19.4, Lab Study A

- compound microscope
- stereoscopic microscope
- preserved lancelet *Amphioxus* (Ward's # 690052) (Call Carolina Biological Supply to check availability.)

  Students do not dissect these, so they can be reused.
- prepared slide *Amphioxus* w.m. (Carolina Biological Supply # 308316, Ward's # 928500)
- prepared slide *Amphioxus* c.s. (composite: Carolina Biological Supply # 308346; or pharyngeal region: Carolina Biological Supply # 308328)

For Each Two Students

Exercise 19.4, Lab Study B

- preserved fetal pig

  Pigs will be used in this lab as well as in Lab Topics 22, 23, and 24. Use large, double-injected fetal pigs. We use formalin-free 11–13 inch pigs purchased from Delta Biologicals (#140.1293.50 for 50). Carolina Biological Supply also offers formalin-free fetal pigs in several sizes. We recommend 11–14 inches, for example: (plain: # 228404, single injected: # 228414, double injected: # 228425–#228426).

Demonstration/Supplies Table

Exercise 19.1

- male *Ascaris* (Have whole and dissected preserved male worms on demonstration if the worms you received from the biological supply house were mostly females.)

Instructor's Desk

- projection technology (computer with digital projector or document camera, or overhead projector)
- photomicroscopy system (optional)

Checklist of Materials

Equipment

For each student

_____ compound microscope (1)
_____ stereoscopic microscope (1)
_____ dissecting instruments (1 set)
_____ dissecting pan (1)
_____ disposable gloves (1 pair)
_____ hand lens (optional) (1)

Live/Prepared Materials

For each student

preserved:
_____ female *Ascaris* (1)
_____ crayfish (1)
_____ grasshopper (1)
_____ sea star
_____ *Amphioxus* (1)
prepared slides of:
_____ *Ascaris* c.s. (1)
_____ *Amphioxus* w.m. (1)
_____ *Amphioxus* c.s. composite (1)

For each two students

_____ preserved fetal pig (1)

Demonstration/Supplies Table

_____ male *Ascaris*

Instructor's Desk

_____ projection technology (computer with digital projector or document camera, or overhead projector)
_____ photomicroscopy system (optional)

LAB TOPIC 20

Plant Anatomy

In this lab, students work independently on prepared slides and work in pairs on plant morphology (Exercise 20.1), to prepare hand sections with the nuts-and-bolts microtomes (Exercise 20.3, Lab Study A), and for Grocery Store Botany (Exercise 20.5). The highlights of this lab are the hand sectioning and the Grocery Store Botany. Prepare samples of various stems for sectioning in advance to allow instructors to view these sections and compare them with the prepared stem slide. Enjoy choosing a variety of produce from local grocers. Provide a list for the instructor before lab!

We have students supply their own blank slides and coverslips. We dispense the prepared slides in numbered plastic slide boxes.

Laboratory instructors may find it helpful to include microscopic projection of prepared slides of *Cucurbita* (pumpkin) stem c.s. and l.s. when introducing the lab topic. This may also be used to assist students in locating and orienting structures as they study other microscope slides. Take care, however, that students do not rely on projected images rather than observing their own slides.

For Each Student

- compound microscope

Exercise 20.2

- prepared slide of *Coleus* stem l.s. (Carolina Biological Supply # 302918 is a near-median section)

Exercise 20.3, Lab Study A

- prepared slide of dicot stem (annual dicot stem, Triarch # T-11H) The prepared slide of *Medicago sativa* (alfalfa) stem c.s. (Carolina Biological Supply # 302780) used in previous editions may still be used, but the Triarch slide is superior.

Exercise 20.3, Lab Study B

- prepared slide of *Ranunculus* root c.s. (Carolina Biological Supply # 302090)
- 2 colored pencils

Exercise 20.3, Lab Study C

- prepared slide of lilac leaf c.s. (Carolina Biological Supply # 303790; # 303838 is a c.s. of a privet leaf showing the mid-vein)
- leaves of purple heart (*Setcreasia*), one in DI water, the other in saline solution

Exercise 20.4
- prepared slide of basswood, *Tilia* stem c.s. (Carolina Biological Supply # 302840)

For Each Two Students

Exercise 20.1
- living bean or geranium plant
- squirt bottle of water
- paper towels

Exercise 20.3, Lab Study A
- petri dish of 50% ethanol
- dropper bottles of:
    DI water
    50% glycerine
    toluidine blue stain
- microscope slides
- coverslips
- forceps
- single-edge razor blade (For best results, use only once.)
- nut-and-bolt microtome
- melted paraffin (keep in paraffin oven)

Exercise 20.3, Lab Study C
- dropper bottle of saline solution

Demonstration/Supplies Table

prepared slides of *Cucurbita* (pumpkin) stem, c.s. and l.s. (optional for microscopic projection) (Carolina Biological Supply # 303062 [c.s.] and # 303068 [l.s.])

Exercise 20.3, Lab Study A
- paraffin oven at 58°C (to keep beakers of paraffin warm)

Exercise 20.3, Lab Study B
- demonstration of:
    fibrous root system (grass)
    taproot system (dandelion, pine seedling, carrot)

Exercise 20.5
- variety of produce, including squash, lettuce, celery, carrot, white potato, sweet potato, asparagus, onion, broccoli, eggplant, brussels sprouts still on the stalk, rhubarb

Instructor's Desk
- projection technology (computer with digital projector or document camera, or overhead projector)
- photomicroscopy system (optional)

Greenhouse Supplies

- living bean plants or geranium plants (Exercise 20.1)

  Bean plants should be started from seed 4 weeks before lab. These bean plants can also be used for preparing the stem sections in paraffin. Carolina Biological Supply offers a variety of seeds (# 158403 for pinto beans) or purchase from a local feed store.

- plants with young stems for preparing stem sections in paraffin (Exercise 20.3, Lab Study A)

  Try germinating beans or other seeds. Sunflower seedlings do not work well. We have had excellent results with pig weed (lambsquarters) (*Chenopodium album*) seedlings, but we have not been able to find a commercial source. Each flower produces many seeds, however, so if you can find even one plant, you will have seeds for many seedlings. This plant is found throughout the United States and may become weedy or invasive, but it is great for this lab activity. Young stems from mature plants also work well. Try *Coleus,* for example.

- *Setcreasia,* purple heart (Exercise 20.3, Lab Study C)

  This plant can be easily grown from cuttings. See leaf preparation under Materials Preparation Notes.

Grocery Supplies

- a variety of produce representatives of plant structures

  Be creative! Select produce from farmers' and specialty markets. Label each item with its plant name. See the previous list for suggestions.

Solution Preparation Notes

50% Ethanol

Add 50 mL of 95% ethanol to a 100-mL graduated cylinder. Add DI water up to 95 mL.

50% Glycerine

Add equal volumes of glycerine (glycerol: Carolina Biological Supply # 865530) and DI water to make this 50% glycerine solution. You will need approximately 1 mL per pair of students.

Toluidine Blue

The easiest way to make a solution of this stain is by simply adding the toluidine blue O powder (Carolina Biological Supply # 896638) to DI water. We have read several different concentrations in different publications and have found that almost any concentration works. Just vary the time in the stain to obtain the best intensity. We suggest staining with a 0.2% solution for 10–15 seconds (as described in the lab manual). To make a 0.2% solution, add 0.2 grams of toluidine blue O to 100 mL water. Try this before lab, and if the sections are too dark, dilute the 0.2% solution to 0.05% by adding 25 mL of the 0.2% solution to 75 mL water.

Materials Preparation Notes

Nuts-and-Bolts Microtomes

Purchase nuts and bolts at any hardware store. Nuts should be 0.5 in. deep and have an internal diameter of 0.5 in. Bolts should fit the nuts and be flat-headed so the microtome can be placed on a flat surface. Use *Coleus*, sunflower (*Helianthus*), or bean (*Phaseolus vulgaris*) plants to obtain 0.5-in. sections of primary stem or lateral branches for embedding in paraffin (see notes under Greenhouse Supplies). Be sure to use new growth, as old growth may have developed a continuous band of vascular cambium rather than separate vascular bundles. Try this ahead of time and compare with the figure in the laboratory manual.

Use paraffin with a melting point of 50-56°C. Fisher Scientific offers Paraplast with the melting point 50-54°C (# 23-021-399). We use Paraplast® (Carolina Biological Supply # 879190). For best results, melt the paraffin in a paraffin warming oven at about 58°C. Have a heat-resistant glove beside the oven for students to use to hold the beaker.

If you do not have a warming oven, place the paraffin in a 100-mL beaker. Nest the 100-mL beaker of paraffin inside a 250-mL beaker of water, and place it on a hot plate to melt the paraffin. Paraffin is flammable and should not be heated directly on a hot plate.

When students embed their stems they should barely screw the nuts onto the bolts, leaving the maximum depth inside the nut. Cut 0.5-in.-long sections of stem, making the cuts as perpendicular to the stem as possible. Place each piece of stem upright into the nut. Pour paraffin into the nut covering the section of stem. Be sure to cover the tip of the stem with paraffin to prevent desiccation. Allow the paraffin to harden (15–20 minutes). Do not attempt to speed up this process with cold water or ice as the sections may be damaged. Paraffin is very difficult to remove from beakers, so plan to use the same beakers year after year. Pour the melted paraffin out of the beaker before storage, however. If the paraffin hardens, it will crack the beaker. The nuts and bolts can be cleaned with xylene after use.

Purple Heart (*Setcreasia*)

To prepare *Setcreasia* leaves to study stomata, remove healthy leaves from the plant 1 hour before lab. (Two students may share one pair of leaves.) Place one leaf for every two students in DI water in a small labeled finger bowl. Place one leaf for every two students in a saline solution (about 1%) in a labeled finger bowl. Keep these bowls on the demonstration table. At the appropriate time, students should take the leaves (one for each pair) to their study area to prepare the slides.

Checklist of Materials

Equipment

For each student

_____ compound microscope (1)
_____ colored pencils (2)

For each two students

_____ paper towels (1 stack)
_____ microscope slides (1 box)
_____ coverslips (1 box)
_____ forceps (2 pairs)

_____ single-edge razor blade (1)
_____ nut-and-bolt microtome (1)
_____ small petri dish with 50% EtOH (1)

Demonstration/Supplies Table

For each class

_____ paraffin oven (1) with several small beakers of melted paraffin
_____ heat-resistant glove to handle beakers of paraffin (1–2)
_____ fibrous root system (grass) (1)
_____ taproot system (dandelion, pine seedling, or carrot) (1)
_____ variety of produce (1 of each)
_____ prepared slides of *Cucurbita* stem, c.s., l.s. (optional)

Instructor's Desk

_____ projection technology (computer with digital projector or document camera, or overhead projector)
_____ photomicroscopy system (optional)

Greenhouse Supplies

For each student

_____ purple heart leaf in DI water
_____ purple heart leaf in saline
_____ plants for stem sections

For each two students

_____ living bean or geranium plant (1)

Solutions/Chemicals

For each two students

_____ small petri dish of 50% ethanol (1)
_____ wash bottle of water (1)
dropper bottles of:
_____ DI water (1)
_____ 50% glycerine (1)
_____ toluidine blue stain (1)
_____ 1% saline

Live/Prepared Materials

For each student

prepared slides of:
_____ *Coleus* stem tip l.s. (1)
_____ typical herbaceous dicot stem c.s. (1)
_____ *Ranunculus* root c.s. (1)
_____ lilac leaf c.s. (1)
_____ basswood *Tilia* stem c.s. (1)

LAB TOPIC 21

Plant Growth

This exercise requires that students first perform a short demonstration experiment (Experiment A of each exercise). Then they work in teams to design and perform an additional experiment, choosing one of the options presented (Experiment B of each exercise). All materials in the Experiment A materials list should be available. You may choose to vary the materials for the Experiment B activities depending on the availability of seeds and living plants. In addition, students may request additional materials. If possible, encourage independent ideas by supplying additional materials as requested. Prepare a PowerPoint slide or write on the board a list of all available materials for the student-designed investigations. New in this edition, we have included a template that can be used to assist student teams in developing their proposals. Using a template will simplify evaluating their proposals and preparing the materials needed for their open-inquiry investigations.

For Each Student

Exercise 21.1, Experiment A
- germinating lima bean seeds (seeds, Carolina Biological Supply # 158335)
- petri dishes with germinating *Brassica rapa* seeds (seeds, Carolina Biological Supply # 158804 for 50 seeds, 158805 for 200 seeds) (Two students can share one dish.)
- stereoscopic microscope or hand lens

For Each Four Students

- computer with Table 21.1 downloaded in Excel format from www.masteringbiology.com

Exercise 21.3, Experiment A
- 2 pots of tall (normal) corn seedlings (one treated with water, one treated with gibberellin) (seeds, Carolina Biological Supply # 159243)
- 2 pots of dwarf corn seedlings (one treated with water, one treated with gibberellin) (seeds, Carolina Biological Supply # 177110)
- rulers
- calculators (Students supply their own.)

Demonstration/Supplies Table

Exercise 21.2, Experiment A
- *Coleus* plant placed on its side

  Plant two to three *Coleus* plants in glass jars so that students can see the roots respond to gravity. Carefully place the jars on their sides at least 1 week before lab.
- *Coleus* plant in unilateral light

About 1–2 weeks before lab, place two to three *Coleus* plants in a dark place, and shine light from one side only.

- *Coleus* plant in upright position

Place two to three *Coleus* plants in normal upright positions and normal light conditions to serve as controls.

Instructor's Desk

- projection technology (computer with digital projector or document camera, or overhead projector)
- Table 21.1 downloaded in Excel format from www.masteringbiology.com. Select Instructor Resources, Instructor Guides for Supplements, and then Data Tables from Investigating Biology Lab Manual, 9e. Students can record their data and analyze the results.
- USB drive

Supplies for Student-Designed Investigations: Exercise 21.4

The following items may be available for the student-designed investigations. Have these supplies in an area of the lab separated from the supplies for Experiments A in each exercise, the required activities and demonstrations.

Exercise 21.1, Experiment B

- *Brassica rapa* seeds and seedlings: wild type (Carolina Biological Supply # 158804 or # 158805); rosette (Carolina Biological Supply # 158815 is a gibberellin-deficient mutant); petite (Carolina Biological Supply # 158832 is NOT a gibberellin-deficient mutant.)
- various other seeds (bean, corn, radish, black locust, mimosa, okra) obtained from a seed store or a biological supply house
- 35-mm film canisters (clear plastic, black with no holes, or black with holes punched in the sides)

Check with film processing establishments. They discard film canisters and are happy to give them to you. These can also be purchased online in packs of 15 in clear or black from Amazon.com.

- hole punch
- 24 small squares of blotting paper soaked in water (Be sure this is blotting paper, not filter paper.)
- floral foam disks 28 mm diameter, 2–4 mm thick, soaking in water (an alternative to blotting paper)

To make these, cut foam cylinders from sheets of floral foam: Cut the bottom off of a Fuji brand film canister, and bevel the outside edge with a knife. Press this canister through a dry floral foam block to cut out a cylinder. With a flat knife, slice disks of foam 2–4 mm thick from the cylinders. These disks should fit into the film canisters used for investigations. (This information is from the Fast Plants website.)

- red, green, and blue plastic light filters

Use the same filters that you used in Lab Topic 6, Photosynthesis. Red, blue, and green filters may be purchased from Barn Door Lighting Outfitters. We recommend that you purchase Rosco filters from this vendor. To transmit blue wavelengths, we recommend Rosco Cinegel # R362S (transmits 32% at 480 nm). For green, choose Rosco Cinegel R386S (32% transmittance at 530 nm). For red, choose Rosco Cinegel # R324S (31% transmittance at 660-700 nm).

- grid sheets to fit petri dish lids
- wick and grid germination strips
- 2 sets of forceps
- 2 scissors
- 2 waterproof pens
- 4 agar plates
- 4 plastic petri dishes
- pH solutions
- NaCl and DI water
- sucrose and DI water
- 1 balance
- 1 roll labeling tape
- 8 small screw-cap jars for students to prepare and take solutions home with them for daily applications
- water bath
- oven
- sandpaper
- reservoirs
- soluble fertilizers
- Osmocote NPK solid fertilizer pellets
- 10% sodium hyperchlorite solution (500 mL)
- solutions of gibberellin and/or other hormones (e.g., abscisic acid cytokinins, brassinosteroids, and jasmonic acid) in several concentrations

Exercise 21.2, Experiment B

- auxin solutions of various concentrations (auxin powder Sigma-Aldrich # 12886)
- auxin in lanolin paste
- lanolin with no auxin (control)
- 2,4 dichlorophenoxyacetic acid (2,4-D) herbicide solution
- scissors
- 2 *Coleus* plants

   Coleus plants can be purchased at your local nursery in the spring and late summer, or you can obtain them from biological supply houses (Carolina Biological Supply # 157310 or 157312).

- 4 quads of *Brassica rapa* seedlings, a total of 16 seedlings (quads, Carolina Biological Supply # 158960)
- 2 corn or bean pots or flats
- 3 day-old *Brassica rapa* seedlings germinated in petri dishes
- *Brassica rapa* seeds
- 35-mm black film canisters
- floral foam disks, 28 mm diameter, 2–4 mm thick, soaking in water
- wick and grid germination strips
- forceps
- red, green, and blue light filter sheets
- 2 gooseneck lamps
- toothpicks
- 2 glass jars for pots
- small plastic pots
- aluminum foil
- protractor or smartphone with protractor app

Angle Pro app will measure angles and can be downloaded for free:
https://itunes.apple.com/us/app/angle-pro/id750327028?mt=8
https://play.google.com/store/apps/details?id=com.FiveFufFive.AngleProFreeAndroid

Exercise 21.3, Experiment B

- gibberellin-deficient dwarf *Brassica rapa* seedlings (rosette seeds are gibberellin-deficient, Carolina Biological Supply # 158815; petite seeds are not gibberellin-deficient, Carolina Biological Supply # 158832); *Brassica rapa* mutant tall ein/ein (Carolina Biological Supply # 158824 for 50 seeds or # 158825 for 200 seeds)
- normal and dwarf corn seedlings
- normal pea seedlings (Carolina Biological Supply # 158863)
- dwarf pea seedlings (Little Marvel peas, *Pisum sativum,* Carolina Biological Supply # 158883)
- solutions of gibberellin
- dropper bottles
- sprayers
- cotton-tipped applicators
- chlorocholine chloride (CCC-commercially known as Cyocel™), various concentrations (a plant growth retardant) (Sigma-Aldridge # C4049)

Preparation of Seeds and Seedlings

Germinating lima bean, corn, pea seeds, Exercise 21.1, Experiments A and B

If seeds have not been pretreated to inhibit fungal growth, wash pea, corn, and bean seeds in a 10% household bleach solution to kill bacterial and fungal spores on their surfaces before planting. Rinse thoroughly with distilled water. Soak pea and corn seeds in DI water overnight before planting. If corn, bean, or pea seeds are to be germinated for extended growth, plant seeds ½ inch deep in flats of vermiculite. Add water or test solution to the flats daily. Seedlings may be transplanted to potting soil in smaller containers for distribution to students. Seeds for Exercise 21.1, Experiment A, can be germinated between wet paper towels. Begin germination 2–3 days before needed. Keep moist.

Notes about seeds for Exercise 21.1, Experiment B

- Okra seeds may respond differently to different temperature regimes.
- Mimosa and black locust seeds must be scarified to germinate. Sandpaper may be used for scarification.

Germinating *B. rapa* seeds in petri dishes, Exercise 21.1, Experiments A and B

We recommend that you purchase the *Wisconsin Fast Plants Manual and Growing Instructions,* published by Carolina Biological Supply, and follow its instructions for germinating *B. rapa* seeds and growing seedlings. Brief instructions follow, which may be adequate for the prep of this lab topic.

To germinate *B. rapa* seeds, you will need a water reservoir, petri dishes, filter paper the size of the petri dish, and seeds. You could use the bottom of a 2-L soft drink bottle for the water reservoir. We use large plastic cups used to serve ice cream. Place the filter paper in the lid of the petri dish. Add DI water to moisten. Lightly press 3–4 seeds on the paper in a neat row. Add DI water to the water reservoir, and place the petri dish on its end in the water (see Figure 21.2 in the lab manual). Check the level of water in the reservoir daily. Keep about 2 cm of water in the reservoir. Begin germination about 48 hours before the plants are needed.

If students germinate *B. rapa* seeds in petri dishes for their original experiment, they may need to measure the rate of growth of the seedlings. An easy way to do this is to tape a metric grid to the outside of the petri dish lid. To make these grids, make an acetate photocopy of a piece of graph paper with the appropriate grid size (0.5-cm intervals work well). Cut this to the size of the petri dish and tape it to the outside of the lid.

Germinating *Brassica rapa* seedlings in quads, Exercise 21.2, Experiment B; Exercise 21.3, Experiment B

See instructions for germinating *B. rapa* seedlings in quads in Lab Topic 8, Mendelian Genetics I: Fast Plants.

To study the effects of gibberellin, Exercise 21.3, Experiment A

For each team, prepare four pots as follows:

pot 1: normal corn, water treatment
pot 2: normal corn, gibberellin treatment
pot 3: dwarf corn, water treatment
pot 4: dwarf corn, gibberellin treatment

Plant the dwarf or normal corn seeds in clay or plastic pots using potting soil. Plant more than four seeds about 1 inch apart and ½ inch deep at least 3–4 weeks before lab. The dwarf corn takes longer to germinate, so you must plant these seeds 1 week before planting the normal corn. Water all plants daily with distilled water. Before treating, thin plants to four per pot. Spray the plants in pots 2 and 4 with gibberellic acid solution (instructions for preparation below) twice during the week before lab. Occasionally the dwarf corn seeds do not germinate well or are not available. We recommend that you order early and try germinating a few of the seeds before you begin the germinations for lab. If the corn seeds do not germinate, substitute dwarf and normal peas.

Dwarf and normal pea seeds are also available and can be substituted for corn in this exercise: normal = Alaska (Carolina Biological Supply # 158863) and dwarf = Little Marvel (Carolina Biological Supply # 158883). We prefer corn to peas because students find it easier to measure corn plants. However, pea germination is more rapid and much more reliable than dwarf corn germination. One year when *none* of the dwarf corn seeds germinated, we germinated peas and were able to save the experiment.

Growing *B. rapa* seedlings in film canisters for tropism studies, Exercise 21.2, Experiment B, and Exercise 21.3, Experiment B.

Preparing wick and grid germination strips:

- To make **grid strips**, photocopy millimeter square graph paper onto an overhead transparency sheet. Cut the sheet along the lines to make strips with the dimensions 0.5 cm x 4 cm.
- Make **wick strips** by cutting blotting paper or folded paper towels into strips with the dimensions 0.5 cm x 4 cm.
- Hold a wick strip with a grid strip aligned on top of it. Place in a Petri dish or other flat container and use a pipette to moisten the wick strips. As the wick becomes moist, the grid will adhere to it. Together, the wick and grid make a **germination strip**. A moist germination strip will adhere to the wall of a film canister. The grid can be used to measure changes in the growing plants.

- To grow seeds or seedlings in the canister, place the germination strip in the canister with the grid strip between the wick and the side of the can. Add a small amount of water and have the wick in contact with the water in the film canister. (See Figure 21.4 in the laboratory manual.)
- Some studies will require that the canister be in the dark and on its side. After the experiment is set up, mark which side is up. Tape the canister to another lid to keep it from rolling.
- For gravitropism studies, students can stick a seedling to the wick strip with the cotyledons against the wick and the hypocotyls pointing out into the canister. (See Figure 21.4 in the laboratory manual.) Students will have other ideas for questions that might be investigated while growing seeds or seedlings in chambers with germination strips.

For additional instructions on making growth chambers and maintaining plants for experiments, see www.fastplants.org/pdf/activities/.

Schedule for Plants and Seeds

4 weeks before lab: Begin germinating the dwarf corn.

3 weeks before lab: Begin germinating the normal corn.

3 weeks before lab: Begin germinating the Little Marvel peas, both dwarf and normal.

11 days before lab: Plant *B. rapa* seeds in quads to be available for student experiments.

10 days–2 weeks before lab: Prepare *Coleus* for gravitropism and phototropism demonstrations. Germinate radish seeds in small pots.

Last week before lab: Spray corn with gibberellic acid solution. Seven days before lab, begin germinating lima beans in flats of vermiculite for Exercise 21.1. Germinate radish seeds on filter paper in petri dishes.

48 hours before lab: Germinate *B. rapa* seeds for Exercise 21.1 on filter paper in petri dishes.

Solution Preparation Notes

pH Solutions, Exercise 21.1, Experiment B

Have available several solutions of buffers at different pHs for students to choose from. We suggest pH 10, 8, 7, 5.6 ("normal" rain pH), and 3 (typical acid rain pH).

These pH solutions might include a 1% acetic acid (add 1 mL acetic acid to 100 mL DI water) and a 1% NaOH solution (add 1 g NaOH to 100 mL DI water) in addition to the series of buffers. Premixed buffers can be purchased from chemical/biological supply houses and prepared according to package directions.

Additional Growth Regulators, Exercise 21.1, Experiment B

Growth regulators: abscisic acid (Sigma # A1049), cytokinin (kinetin, Sigma # K0753), jasmonic acid (methyl jasmonate, Sigma #392707), brassinosteroid (epibrassinolide, Sigma # E1641) must first be mixed with a small amount of 95% ethanol before diluting with distilled water. See additional information on the Sigma website: http://www.sigmaaldrich.com/technical-documents/protocols/biology/growth-regulators.html.

Auxin Solutions, Exercise 21.2, Experiment B

Dissolve auxin (indole-3-acetic acid) powder (Sigma-Aldrich # 12886) in DI water. Make a stock of 10^{-4} M stock solution (17.52 mg/L) and dilute to desired concentrations. You might also make up a more concentrated solution. Generally, 0.5% (5000 ppm) and 0.05% (500 ppm) solutions are used to check growth regulators. To make a lanolin/auxin paste: make a 1% auxin/lanolin mixture (1% [w/w]). For example, mix 0.1 g auxin in 10 g lanolin. Lanolin can be purchased from a pharmacy or drug store, or from Sigma-Aldrich # L7387.

2,4 Dichlorophenoxyacetic Acid (2,4-D) Solutions, Exercise 21.2, Experiment B

Available from commercial sources (horticulture supplies), this synthetic auxin is water soluble.

Begin with a 0.2% solution (0.2 g/100 mL H_2O) and have students prepare dilutions (1:2, 1:4, etc.)

Caution students to spray their experimental plants outside and away from all other experimental plants. Designate sprayers for use with 2,4-D only.

Gibberellic Acid Solution (GA), Exercise 21.3, Experiment A

Mix 0.175 g of GA (Sigma-Aldrich # G1025) in a few drops of 95% ethanol. Add a small amount of H_2O to mix. Then bring the volume up to 500 mL with DI water. Gibberellic acid from Sigma-Aldridge is very expensive. Search online for other vendors.

Gibberellin Solutions, Exercise 21.3, Experiment B

Prepare solutions more and less concentrated than the GA solution used in Experiment A.

Agar Plates

Prepare nutrient agar plates as instructed in the prep for Lab Topic 12. Have plain agar powder available for students to use if they choose to prepare agar plates with different nutrients in the medium for their experiment.

Checklist of Materials

Equipment

For each student

_____ stereoscopic microscope or hand lens (1)
_____ ruler (1)
_____ calculator (students should supply their own) (1)

Live/Prepared Materials

For each student

_____ germinating lima bean seeds (1)
_____ petri dish of germinating *Brassica rapa* seeds (1 for each student or for each two students)

For each four students

_____ dwarf corn (1 water-treated, 1 GA-treated) (2 pots)
_____ normal corn (1 water-treated, 1 GA-treated) (2 pots)

Demonstration/Supplies Table (Required for Experiment A)

For each class

_____ *Coleus* plant placed on its side (1)
_____ *Coleus* plant in unilateral light (1)
_____ *Coleus* plant in upright position (1)

Demonstration/Supplies Table (For Student-Designed Investigations)

For each class

Seedlings:
_____ *Brassica rapa*, wild type (4 quads)
_____ *Brassica rapa*, rosette (4 quads)
_____ normal corn seedlings (4 pots)
_____ dwarf corn seedlings (4 pots)
_____ normal pea seedlings (2 pots)
_____ dwarf pea seedlings (2 pots)
_____ *Coleus* plants (2 pots)

Seeds:
_____ *Brassica rapa* (several)
_____ lima bean, *Phaseolus limensis* (several)
_____ pinto bean, *Phaseolus vulgaris* (several)
_____ corn, *Zea mays* (several)
_____ mimosa (several)
_____ okra (several)
_____ black locust (several)

Chemicals/growth supplies:
_____ auxin in lanolin paste (1 container)
_____ lanolin with no auxin (1 container)
_____ auxin solutions
_____ 2,4-D solutions
_____ gibberellin (GA) solutions
_____ agar plates (4)
_____ plastic petri dishes (4)
_____ 1% acetic acid
_____ 1% NaOH
_____ buffer solutions
_____ NaCl
_____ sucrose
_____ DI water
_____ soluble fertilizer
_____ Osmocote NPK fertilizer pellets
_____ 10% sodium hyperchlorite solution
_____ other growth regulator solutions

Equipment:

_____ 35-mm film canisters, clear plastic (4)
_____ 35-mm film canisters, black, no holes (4)
_____ 35-mm film canisters, black, with holes punched in the sides (4)
_____ small squares of blotting paper soaking in water (24)
_____ foam disks soaking in water (optional)
_____ squares of red, green, and blue plastic filters (2 each)
_____ grid sheets to fit petri dish lids (4)
_____ germination disks (wicks and grids)
_____ forceps (2)
_____ scissors (2)
_____ waterproof pen (2)
_____ labeling tape, roll (1)
_____ balance (1)
_____ small screw-cap jars (8)
_____ lamps (2)
_____ toothpicks (10)
_____ glass jars for pots (2)
_____ aluminum foil, roll (1)
_____ dropper bottles (4)
_____ plant sprayers (2)
_____ cotton-tipped applicators (8)
_____ water bath
_____ oven
_____ sandpaper
_____ reservoirs
_____ protractor or smartphone with protractor app

Instructor's Desk

For each class

_____ projection technology (computer with digital projector or document camera, or overhead projector)
_____ Table 21.1 downloaded in Excel format from www.masteringbiology.com
_____ USB drive

Plant Growth and Development Research Proposal

Team Name: **Team Members:**

Date: **Instructor:**

Question:

Hypothesis:

Prediction:

Summary of the Procedures:

Materials:

Think about additional materials or supplies that you will need for your experiment. List those here. Include in your materials any instruments or other lab equipment you will need for preparing your solutions, potting plants, or an area for treatment or observation.

LAB TOPIC 22

Vertebrate Anatomy I:
The Skin and Digestive System

Ideally, each student should dissect a fetal pig, but urge students to compare their pigs with those of their partners. Distribute pigs so that the sexes are approximately 50-50. Students should view all slides independently and discuss observations with their lab partners. As students study slides in the vertebrate anatomy labs, laboratory instructors may find it helpful to have a photomicroscopy system available to assist students in locating and orienting structures. Take care, however, that students do not rely on projected images rather than observing their own slides.

For Each Student

Exercise 22.1
- compound microscope
- prepared slide of mammalian skin, pig, monkey, or human. Carolina Biological Supply # 314522 (human), 314504 (rat or pig, showing hair follicles); Triarch # HI1-21 (human non-pigmented), HI1-22 (human pigmented), HI1-3 (mammalian skin with hair follicles), HI1-23 (human skin scalp), Ward's # 935023 (skin of hairy mammal). We suggest you sample several of these before you purchase larger numbers for your class.

  Sweat glands are more common in pig skin; sebaceous glands are more common in monkey skin. If possible, have both available.

Exercise 22.2
- disposable gloves

  We ask students to supply their own gloves. If you provide them, choose from the selection of gloves from VWR Scientific # 32916, or from the selection beginning at Carolina Biological Supply # 706337.

- dissecting instruments (2 dissecting needles, good quality scissors, blunt probe, forceps, scalpel, small metric ruler)

  Students use the same personal dissecting kit that they purchased for the animal diversity labs (Lab Topics 18 and 19).

- preserved fetal pig (order large, 11–13 in., double-injected fetal pigs, Carolina Biological Supply # 228424-#228426). Call early about availability.

  We use formalin-free pigs purchased from Delta Biologicals (# 140.1293.50 for 50) 11-13 inches, double-injected.

- dissecting pan
- 2 lengths of twine to tie pigs open in dissecting pans

Exercise 22.3

- preserved fetal pig
- stereoscopic microscope or hand lens
- plastic specimen bag (Ward's # 18W-6940) with twist ties and two labels
- prepared slide of small intestine c.s. (Carolina Biological Supply # 312402 or # 315226 [ileum])

Demonstration/Supplies Table

- box of disposable gloves (if students do not supply their own)
- preservative
- ball of twine
- disposal container marked "organic waste only" (We use large plastic buckets.)
- container to store pigs

Instructor's Desk

- projection technology (computer with digital projector or document camera, or over-head projector)
- photomicroscopy system (optional)

Solution Preparation Notes

Preservative

If pigs come shipped in preservative, keep this to pour into individual pig bags at the end of each lab. If you do not have preservative, you can order Carosafe concentrate preservative (Carolina Biological Supply # 853353) or use 70% 1-propanol (n-propyl alcohol) obtained from a biological supply house.

Checklist of Materials

Equipment

For each student

_____ compound microscope (1)
_____ stereoscopic microscope or hand lens (1)
_____ dissecting pan (1)
_____ dissecting instruments (1 set)
_____ plastic bag with twist ties and two labels (1)
_____ pieces of twine (2)

Live/Prepared Materials

For each student

_____ preserved fetal pig (1)
_____ prepared slide of mammalian skin (pig or monkey) (1)
_____ prepared slide of small intestine c.s. (1)

Demonstration/Supplies Table

_____ preservative
_____ organic waste disposal container
_____ container to store pigs

_____ ball of twine (1)
_____ disposable gloves (1 box, if students do not supply their own)

Instructor's Desk

_____ projection technology (computer with digital projector or document camera, or overhead projector)
_____ photomicroscopy system (optional)

Vertebrate Anatomy II:
The Circulatory and Respiratory Systems

For Each Student

- preserved fetal pig (see suggested sources of pigs in Lab Topic 22)
- dissecting pan
- dissecting instruments (see Lab Topic 22)
- plastic specimen bag (Ward's # 18W-6940) with twist tie and labels
- 2 lengths of twine to tie pigs open in dissecting pans
- compound microscope (Exercise 23.5)
- prepared slide, smear of human blood (Exercise 23.5) (Carolina Biological Supply # 313158)

Demonstration/Supplies Table

- 3 or 4 preserved or fresh isolated hearts of adult sheep (Carolina Biological Supply # 228771) or pig (Carolina Biological Supply # 228561)

  We prefer pig hearts because of their larger size. However, we do not recommend beef hearts because they are so large that they are difficult to dissect when preserved. Fresh hearts may be available from a local farmers' market or slaughterhouse. They will be easier to dissect and are better representations, but they must be kept on ice during lab and refrigerated between labs. Dissect the demonstration hearts to show internal features of chambers and valves by cutting along a median plane separating the dorsal and ventral halves. Leave the vessels connected at the heart.

- preservative
- box of disposable gloves (choose from the selection of gloves from VWR Scientific # 32916, or from the selection beginning at Carolina Biological Supply # 706337, if students do not supply their own)
- ball of twine
- disposal container marked "for organic waste only"
- container to store pigs
- materials describing/depicting the effects of smoking cigarettes on circulatory and respiratory systems. These can be obtained from libraries and the American Cancer Society. See also the following websites:
  www.nlm.nih.gov/medlineplus/smoking.html
  www.cdc.gov/tobacco/quit_smoking/index.htm
  www.marchofdimes.org/pregnancy/smoking-during-pregnancy.aspx
  www.hhs.gov

  A comprehensive report of the consequences of tobacco use in the United States: 50 years of Progress: A Report of the Surgeon General, 2014.

For photos of healthy lungs and lungs of smokers, do an online search for: smoking lungs photos.

Display selected materials on a bulletin board or on a lab bench.

* sheep pluck dissected to show trachea and bronchi (Carolina Biological Supply # 228831)

Instructor's Desk

* projection technology (computer with digital projector)
* photomicroscopy system (optional, to project the blood slide)

Solution Preparation Notes

Preservative

See suggestions for preservative in Lab Topic 22.

Checklist of Materials

Equipment

For each student

_____ dissecting pan (1)
_____ dissecting instruments (1 set)
_____ plastic specimen bags with twist tie and labels (1)
_____ pieces of twine (2)

Live/Prepared Materials

For each student

_____ preserved fetal pig (1)

Demonstration/Supplies Table

For each class

_____ isolated adult sheep or pig hearts (3–4)
_____ preservative
_____ disposable gloves (1 box, if students do not supply their own)
_____ ball of twine (1)
_____ organic waste disposal container
_____ container to store pigs
_____ literature on the effects of smoking
_____ dissected sheep pluck (optional)

Instructor's Desk

_____ projection technology (computer with digital projector)
_____ photomicroscopy system (optional)

Vertebrate Anatomy III:
The Excretory, Reproductive, and Nervous Systems

In this lab, students work independently on all dissections and slide studies. However, collaboration and discussion should be encouraged as they compare their dissections with their lab partner. A person with a male pig should find a person with a female pig, and the two should demonstrate the structures in Exercise 24.2 to each other. If a photomicroscopy system is available, you may use this to help students find structures on their slides. Take care, however, that students do not rely on projected images rather than observing their own slides. In this edition of the laboratory manual a new lab study has been added to Exercise 24.3, Lab Study C. Overview of Sheep Brain Anatomy. We recommend that you have one whole sheep brain and one half-brain cut in sagittal section for each pair of students. If students are careful not to damage the tissues as they make their observations, you should be able to use these brains for multiple sections. At the end of each laboratory session, examine the brains and replace any that may have been damaged beyond use.

For Each Student

Exercises 24.1 and 24.2
- preserved fetal pig
  See possible sources of fetal pigs in Lab Topic 22.
- dissecting pan
- dissecting instruments (scissors, scalpel, blunt probe, and forceps)
- plastic specimen bag (Ward's # 18W-6940) with twist tie and labels
- 2 pieces of twine for tying pigs open in dissecting pan

Exercise 24.3, Lab Study A
- compound microscope
- prepared slide of nervous tissue (Carolina Biological Supply # 313570, a smear of tissue from the spinal cord)

Exercise 24.3, Lab Study B
- stereoscopic microscope
- prepared slide of spinal cord c.s. (Triarch #s HE2-22 or HE2-223 show the dorsal root ganglion; Triarch # HE 2-21 and Carolina Biological Supply # 313708 show cord structure c.s.)

Exercise 24.3, Lab Study D
- preserved cow or sheep eye (sheep eyes: Carolina Biological Supply # 228760) (Sheep eyes are usually less expensive than cow eyes.)

For Each Two Students

Exercise 24.3, Lab Study C

- one preserved whole sheep brain with meninges removed (Carolina Biological Supply # 228701; # 228747 with hypophysis intact)
- one half sheep brain in sagittal section (Carolina Biological Supply # 228730)

Demonstration/Supplies Table

- isolated adult pig or sheep kidney, triple-injected (Carolina Biological Supply # 228591, pig; # 228804, sheep), (Exercise 24.1)

  Have two or three of these on demonstration. Open at least one of these kidneys along the frontal plane.

- microscope slide of section through the kidney cortex of a mammal (Carolina Biological Supply # 315788; Triarch # HA2-1, HA2-11) (Exercise 24.1)

- preserved pregnant pig uterus dissected to expose several fetal pigs (Carolina Biological Supply # 228600) (Exercise 24.2, Lab Study C)

  If possible, show one fetus with the chorionic vesicle still intact and others with the vesicle opened.

- preserved whole sheep brain with dura mater still intact (Carolina Biological Supply # 228711). If possible, also have a sheep brain with the pituitary gland (hypophysis) still attached. (This is usually lost when the brain is removed from the cranium. Carolina Biological sells brains with the hypophysis still attached: # 228747.) Add explanatory labels to these demonstrations.

- ball of twine
- box of disposable gloves (if students do not supply their own) (choose from the selection of gloves from VWR Scientific # 32916, or Carolina Biological Supply # 706337)
- disposal container marked "for organic waste only"
- container to collect pigs and other organic waste for incineration

  Save the best pigs for the practical exam. Check about appropriate disposal procedures for your institution. We have students remove the pig from the plastic bag and dispose of the drained bag, labels, and twist ties in the regular trash. Because we pay for incineration by weight, we place the pigs on large trays in the fume hoods for several days until they dry out, and then we put them in plastic bags in boxes supplied by the incineration company. We save several hundred dollars each year by drying them out before incineration.

Instructor's Desk

- projection technology (computer with digital projector or document camera, or overhead projector)
- photomicroscopy system (optional)

Checklist of Materials

Equipment

For each student

_____ compound microscope (1)
_____ stereoscopic microscope (1)

_____ dissecting pan (1)
_____ dissecting instruments (1 set)
_____ plastic specimen bag with twist tie and labels (1)
_____ pieces of twine for tying pigs open (2)

Live/Prepared Materials

For each student

prepared slides of:
_____ nervous tissue (1)
_____ spinal cord c.s. (1)
preserved materials:
_____ fetal pig (1)
_____ cow or sheep eye (1)

For each two students

_____ preserved whole sheep brain
_____ preserved sheep brain cut in sagittal section

Demonstration/Supplies Table

For each class

_____ preservative, if needed
_____ ball of twine (1)
_____ disposable gloves (1 box)
_____ organic waste disposal container (1)
_____ container for final disposal of pigs (1)
_____ pregnant pig uterus (1)
_____ adult kidneys (2–3) (optional)
_____ microscope slide of kidney cortex tissue
_____ sheep brain with dura mater intact (1)
_____ sheep brain with hypophysis (pituitary gland) intact (1)

Instructor's Desk

_____ projection technology (computer with digital projector or document camera, or overhead projector)
_____ photomicroscopy system (optional)

Animal Development

In this laboratory, students study comparative development using living specimens (sea urchin, fish, and chick), prepared slides (starfish and chick), and film or video observations (salamander or other amphibian). Students work independently with starfish slides. Have one 16-hour and one 24-hour chick slide and one 48-hour and one 96-hour living chick embryo for each pair of students. Ideally, each team of four students has at least one of each stage of early development in the zebra fish and several embryos in organogenesis and hatched stages. We are particularly pleased that we are able to offer an exercise where students study zebra fish. These organisms are rapidly becoming the organism of choice for vertebrate developmental studies. Many developmental biologists predict that zebra fish will become as important a research organism as *Drosophila* has been for research in genetics and development. A photomicroscopy system may be useful to help students locate some structures in embryos. Take care, however, that students do not rely on projected images rather than observing their own slides.

Students particularly enjoy the lab study "Fertilization in Living Sea Urchins." Although this involves more preparation, we encourage you to include the exercise. We have performed this exercise many times in our own classes, and we believe it will be a valuable addition to your labs.

For Each Student

Exercise 25.1, Lab Study A
- compound microscope
- clean microscope slides and coverslips
- moisture chamber (petri dish with moist filter paper)

Exercise 25.1, Lab Study B
- compound microscope
- prepared slides of starfish development, composite: (Carolina Biological Supply # 311126, # 311132). Ward's # 928255 is a composite of all stages. One composite slide for each student is adequate, although you may choose to have on hand slides with single stages for demonstration purposes. Order these additional slides: for early and late cleavage (Carolina Biological Supply # 311072); blastula (Carolina Biological Supply # 311078); gastrula (Carolina Biological Supply # 311102). Ward's # 928251 is a slide of bipinnaria larvae. You may need this additional slide because the Carolina slides often do not have good bipinnaria larvae.

Exercise 25.3
- stereoscopic microscope
- 2–3 toothpicks

- pasteur pipette and bulb
- depression slide
- paper towels

For Each Two Students

Exercise 25.1, Lab Study A

- sand or glass chips in a small petri dish
- transfer pipettes (one labeled "egg," the other labeled "sperm") cut to make a slightly larger bore
- small clean test tube labeled "egg" containing a suspension of living sea urchin eggs
- small clean test tube labeled "sperm" containing a suspension of living sea urchin sperm

Exercise 25.4

- 1 each prepared slides of:
    16-hour chick (Carolina Biological Supply # 311496)
    24-hour chick (Carolina Biological Supply # 311520) (These slides may be closer to 27-30 hours of incubation, but they still work for neurulation.)
- living chick egg incubated 48 hours
- living chick egg incubated 96 hours
- 2 small (about 11 cm, or 4½ in.) culture dishes (finger bowls)
- 2 flat-tipped (cover glass) forceps (Fisher Scientific # 19-060)
- 2 sharp-pointed scissors
- 2 watch glasses
- disposable pipette with bulb

For Each Four Students

- test-tube rack for sperm and egg tubes (Exercise 25.1)
- 1 of each of the following developmental stages of zebra fish placed in separate, small petri dishes: 2-cell, 4-cell, 8-cell, early and late blastula, gastrula, neurula, organogenesis

    If all stages are not available for each set of four students, place embryos on the demonstration table (see below).

Demonstration/Supplies Table

Exercise 25.1, Lab Study A

all supplies to collect sea urchin eggs and sperm (see Live/Prepared Materials)

Exercise 25.2

- digital projector and computer or interactive whiteboard
    Several excellent videos of amphibian development are now available on YouTube. Do a Web search for "amphibian development." One excellent example—"The Development of a Frog": http://www.youtube.com/watch?v=dXpAbezdOho

- DVD: A *Dozen Eggs,* edited by Rachel Fink. Purchase from Sinauer Associates, Inc., Publishers, Sunderland, MA 01375, 413-549-4300. Covers development in sea urchin, frog, zebra fish, chicken, and several other animals. Product Code: 978-0-87893-181-3
- Look in www.masteringbiology.com, Instructor Resources, Ch. 47, animations and videos, for short time-lapse videos of sea urchin and amphhibian (*Xenopus*) development.

Exercise 25.3

- aquarium with zebra fish, timer, aquarium light, large box (for multiple sections, you will need 2 or 3)
- embryo-rearing solution
- at least 24 zebra fish embryos in various developmental stages (if all stages are not available for each four students)

  Place different stages in individual petri dishes and have students take one to their work area, observe it, and return it to the demonstration table.

Exercise 25.4

- unincubated chicken egg broken into a small culture dish and covered with plastic wrap (refrigerate until just before lab)
- flasks of 0.9% NaCl in a 37°C water bath

Instructor's Desk

- projection technology (computer with digital projector or document camera, or overhead projector)
- photomicroscopy system
- See suggestions for amphibian development videos under "Demonstration/Supplies Table." If you choose the excellent video "A Dozen Eggs," you will need a DVD player.

Solution Preparation Notes

0.5 *M* KCl (used to collect sea urchin gametes)

Dissolve 3.73 g KCl in 100 mL DI water. Adjust pH to 7.1.

0.9% NaCl (used with chicken embryos)

Dissolve 9 g NaCl in 1000 mL DI water. Adjust amounts to suit your needs. Each student will need about 150 mL.

Embryo-Rearing Solution

Purchase concentrate (Carolina Biological Supply # 859450) and reconstitute as directed. Each vial makes 500 mL.

Instant Ocean™

Purchase commercially and mix according to directions on the package. Mix several days before the sea urchins arrive to allow all chemicals to dissolve. Check the salinity (34 ppt) or specific gravity (1.025–1.026) and adjust by adding more salt or water. Maintain the sea urchins in this. Filter some of it to use in the experiments.

Live/Prepared Materials

Obtaining Living Eggs and Sperm from Sea Urchins (Exercise 25.1, Lab Study A)

1. Check with your supplier early in the semester for the availability of fertile sea urchins; they are usually only seasonally available. If fertile sea urchins are not available in your area when you need them, you may be able to order them from a supplier in another region of the country. You should use sea urchins within about 3 days of their arrival from the supplier for best results.

   Order living sea urchins (Carolina Biological # 162949 for sea urchins only or, alternatively, # 162505 is a kit with instructions and most of the supplies needed); (Gulf Specimen Marine Laboratories: *Arbacia* # E-1610 [fertile January–April], *Lytechinus* # E-1620 [fertile May–September]). If you have a saltwater aquarium, keep the sea urchins in clean, aerated seawater (you can use Instant Ocean™) until needed (salinity 34 ppt or 3.4%). When the sea urchins arrive, place them in their bags in the aquarium to equilibrate for about 30 minutes. Then add some water from the aquarium into each bag for about 30 minutes before finally carefully sliding the sea urchins into the water. (A warning: Once we placed our sea urchins directly into the tank and they immediately released their gametes.) If the seawater in the bag with a sea urchin is cloudy, do not add this sea urchin to the tank as it has probably already released its gametes and will stimulate others to release their gametes.

   If you do not have a saltwater aquarium, place the sea urchins into large finger bowls with clean seawater and aeration.

2. Assemble the following in the prep or demonstration area where you will collect eggs and sperm:
   - test-tube rack and an empty 250-mL beaker to hold tubes, pipettes, and various supplies
   - two (or more) sea urchins
   - 2 hypodermic syringes with needles (19–20 gauge)
   - 2–3 sterile petri dishes to collect sperm
   - 4 watch glasses to hold the sea urchins after they are injected until you determine their sex
   - 3–4 small finger bowls with seawater to hold the sea urchins after you have collected gametes (Do not return these to the main tank. You may choose to have another tank for "used" sea urchins.)
   - 2 250-mL beakers ¾ filled with seawater to collect eggs from larger sea urchins
   - 2 150-mL beakers ¾ filled with seawater to collect eggs from smaller sea urchins
   - 50-mL beaker to collect and dilute sperm
   - clean transfer pipettes
   - several labeled tubes for sperm and eggs (as needed for student groups)
   - marking pen

3. Prepare the following solutions:
   - 0.5 M KCl solution, pH 7.1
     Add 3.73 g KCl to 100 mL DI water. Adjust pH to 7.1.
   - Filtered seawater. Use Instant Ocean, but make it well in advance and carefully check the salinity, which should be about 34 ppt (3.4% solution, specific gravity 1.025–1.026).

4. Collect the gametes:
    *   Obtain a sea urchin from the tank.
    *   Fill a syringe (with a new needle) with KCl solution.
    *   Locate the oral (mouth or "underside") surface of the sea urchin. Inject 1–2 mL of KCl through the soft membrane surrounding the mouth of the sea urchin into its body cavity.
    *   Place the sea urchin on a clean watch glass, aboral side down (the "top" of the sea urchin away from the mouth). Gametes will be extruded (usually within 2–5 minutes) from the **gonopore** which is located on the aboral surface opposite the mouth of the animal. When the urchin begins to extrude gametes, determine if they are eggs or sperm. Sperm are milky white in appearance. In *Lytechinus*, eggs are light orange, and in *Arbacia*, eggs are reddish. Each female can spawn 1 million eggs and each male 1 billion sperm.
    *   If the sea urchin is male, transfer it (aboral side down) to a dry, sterile petri dish and collect the sperm there. When a sufficient volume of sperm has been collected, remove the urchin and cover the sperm with the dish lid. Do not dilute the sperm. They may be stored concentrated up to 24 hours in the refrigerator. Prepare sperm for the fertilization experiment by placing 1–2 drops (or more if needed) of concentrated sperm from the petri dish into a small labeled test tube or beaker containing about 10 mL (or more if needed) *cold* filtered seawater. This may then be placed in small, labeled test tubes, one for each pair of students. Use the sperm within 10 minutes after it is diluted for best results.
    *   If the sea urchin is female, invert it (aboral side down) over a clean beaker filled with filtered seawater so the spines suspend it on the lip of the beaker. If the 250-mL beaker is too large to hold the urchin, move it to a 150-mL beaker. The eggs should drain directly from the gonopore into the seawater.
    *   When a sufficient volume of eggs has been collected, dispense several drops of the egg suspension into small labeled test tubes containing 10-mL filtered seawater, one for each pair of students.

Zebra danio

Zebra fish breeding tanks are available from Carolina Biological Supply (# 161937). Although we have not used such a tank, we encourage you to check this out, as well as check other sources such as pet and aquarium supply stores. **Just remember that you must be able to collect the eggs and embryos before the adults eat them.** We include below our instructions for using an aquarium and net liner to obtain embryos. Much of this information will be helpful, even if you do choose to use a manufactured breeding tank.

To rear embryos of *Zebra danio* (zebra fish) you will need the following materials:
*   10–15-gal aquarium (at least 1; we use 2)
*   net liner to fit aquarium (net material, needle, string)
*   lamp or aquarium light
*   24-hour timer for light
*   12 or more zebra fish
*   live or frozen brine shrimp and dried fish food
*   embryo-rearing solution
*   petri dishes (100 mm × 15 mm and 60 mm × 15 mm)
*   ice chest with lid and ice
*   pasteur pipettes and/or plastic dropping pipettes

The zebra fish is a common aquarium fish available from pet stores and from biological supply houses (Carolina Biological Supply # 145564 [12 breeding males] and # 14-5566 [12 breeding females]). You will need about 12 fish per tank: about 8 females, 4 males. Females are noticeably larger and broader than males. These fish spawn at dawn when the day length is 16 hours of light and 8 hours of dark.

Preparing the tank

1. Begin with at least one empty, clean 10–15-gal aquarium.
2. About 1 week before you need the embryos, place the aquarium in a warm room. Add a net liner to the inside of each aquarium (directions to prepare the liner follow) and fill with clean tap water.
3. Attach an aerator. We use an air stone (Carolina Biological Supply # 671794) attached to an air pump (Carolina Biological Supply # 671701) using plastic airline tubing. Any aeration will probably work, but do not use gravel or undergravel filters. There should be nothing on the bottom of the aquarium.
4. Allow the aquarium setup to sit overnight to allow the temperature to equilibrate and to free the water of chlorine. When adding fish, add some water from an established tank to this fresh water.
5. After several days, if the tank becomes dirty, move the fish to a clean tank. Be sure to carry over some of the water from the old tank.

The liner

The purpose of the liner is to keep the fish from eating the eggs as they are being laid. The fish will be inside the net, and as they spawn, the eggs will fall to the bottom of the tank through the net. The male fish deposit sperm, and fertilization takes place in the bottom of the tank. The net allows you to pull the fish to the side and collect the embryos from the aquarium bottom without significantly disturbing the fish and with a minimum of interference from the fish.

To construct the liner: Use a fabric netting material and wash it before using it to remove any toxins. The size of the mesh should allow an egg about 2 mm in diameter to fall through. Do not use screening from a hardware store because of the potential for toxic substances in/on the screen. Cut out five pieces of material and use string to securely sew these pieces together, forming a liner approximately the size and shape of the aquarium, as follows: Cut the bottom approximately the same size and shape as the bottom of the aquarium (a rectangle). Cut the four side pieces in the shape of trapezoids. Sew the pieces together using a large needle and string. The finished net liner should be approximately the same shape as the tank, but should widen at the top and be taller than the tank so that it can be folded over the edges of the top of the tank to keep it in place.

Place the liner inside the tank. Secure the liner by draping the edges over the top edges of the tank. You may need to add weights (rocks or marbles) to the inside corners of the liner to hold it down in the right position. After the liner is in place and the water has aged, add the fish.

If you do not have multiple lab sections on multiple days, you can simplify egg collection by using a breeding trap with a bottom grid that allows eggs to fall through, out of reach of the adults. Look for clear acrylic traps at your local pet store. These traps attach inside your fish tank by clips. Place two females and one or two males in the breeding trap the day before you need the eggs. After the eggs have been deposited, remove the adults, being careful not to disturb the eggs. Use a transfer pipette to collect the eggs.

Establishing the light/dark cycle

The fish must be placed on the light/dark cycle 2 days before you need to collect the eggs. For a Monday lab, begin timing the cycle on Friday evening.

1. Place a lamp over the tank and plug it into the timer. Use the timer to set the lamp for 16 hours of light, 8 hours of dark. We set our timer for the light to come on at 8:00 A.M.
2. Place a large box over the aquarium *and light* to prevent unwanted exposure to light.

Collecting the eggs

1. The fish begin to lay eggs shortly after the light comes on. Allow them to lay eggs for about 1 hour before feeding. Shine a light from the back of the tank to facilitate seeing the eggs and early embryos.
2. Gather the fish enclosed in the net liner to one side of the tank. Looking from the front of the tank, use a plastic dropping pipette to stir up the fertilized eggs/embryos on the tank bottom. The embryos will float up. As you see an embryo, quickly pick it up with the pipette and place it into a petri dish half-filled with aquarium water. Continue until you have several embryos. The embryos are usually more concentrated in the corners of the aquarium.
3. Observe the embryos on a dissecting microscope. As you determine the particular stage of development of each embryo, place that embryo in a small petri dish in embryo-rearing solution. The first embryos should be in early cleavage. We put some of these on ice to slow development, and we allow others to continue development at room temperature to have a diversity of stages for students to observe at lab time.
4. To have available embryos at different stages, you must collect embryos at different times and place some of each batch on ice to arrest their development. Use a cold box half-filled with ice. Place a metal or porcelain pan on the ice in the box, and place a thin cloth or several paper towels in the bottom of the pan. Moisten the towels and place the petri dishes with the embryos on the towels. We have found that placing the petri dishes directly on the pan surface kills the embryos. Cover the cold box with the lid.
5. After a couple of hours, collect embryos again and repeat the procedure. If you set your cycle to begin at 8:00 A.M., by an afternoon lab time, you should have an assortment of different developmental stages.
6. To collect embryos every day for a week of labs, have three aquaria. Start the light cycle for one aquarium on the Friday before the lab week begins to have embryos for the Monday and Tuesday labs. Start the light cycle for the second aquarium on Monday for the Wednesday and Thursday labs, and the third aquarium on Wednesday for the Friday lab. You may be able to use only two aquaria and collect embryos from the first for Monday, Tuesday, and Wednesday labs and the second for Thursday and Friday labs. We do not recommend having only one aquarium, however. After several days on the light cycle, the fish stop spawning. Be sure to keep the aquaria clean. Fungi kill the embryos.
7. Be sure the fish are well fed. We purchase live brine shrimp from a pet store to feed them each morning (after allowing them to spawn for about 1 hour). In the evening we feed them dried fish food. For best results, feed them twice daily, including the weekend. Begin the supplemental feeding about 1 week before you begin collecting eggs.

Chick Eggs

Obtain fertile chicken eggs from local suppliers or order them from a biological supply house (Carolina Biological Supply # 139295). Frequently, when we have ordered from Carolina, many of the eggs have not developed. Quail eggs (Carolina Biological Supply # 139330) can be substituted if chick eggs are not available. Again, not all will develop. *It is best to find a local supplier of fertile eggs.* Incubate eggs in an egg incubator at about 100°F (37°C). If your department does not have one, you may be able to substitute an all-purpose 37°C incubator. Be sure to keep a pan of water in the incubator, and if you use an all-purpose incubator, try to rig a small fan inside to circulate the air to prevent CO_2 buildup. Incubate the eggs on end at first, turning them to the other end every day. The day before the eggs will be used, turn them on their side if this is possible (it is not absolutely necessary) so that students can crack the egg on the side away from the embryo.

Checklist of Materials

Equipment

For each student

_____ compound microscope (1)
_____ microscope slides and coverslips
_____ stereoscopic microscope (1)
_____ moisture chamber
_____ toothpicks (2–3)
_____ disposable pasteur pipette (1)
_____ pipette bulb (1)
_____ paper towels
_____ depression slide (1)
_____ culture dish (1)
_____ flat-tipped forceps (1)
_____ sharp-pointed scissors (1)
_____ watch glass (1)

For each two students

_____ sand or glass chips
_____ "egg" and "sperm" transfer pipettes

Demonstration/Supplies Table

For each class

_____ developmental stages of zebra fish in petri dishes (if not enough for 1 set for each four students)
_____ embryo-rearing solution
_____ 37°C water bath
_____ 0.9% NaCl
_____ 2–3 aquaria, each with light, timer, and box, or a zebra fish breeding tank
_____ zebra fish
_____ unincubated chicken egg in culture dish

Instructor's Desk

_____ projection technology (computer with digital projector or document camera, or overhead projector)
_____ photomicroscopy system
_____ supplies to obtain gametes from living sea urchins
_____ living sea urchins
_____ DVD or YouTube video of amphibian development

Grocery Supplies
_____ unincubated chicken eggs

Live/Prepared Materials

For each student

_____ prepared slide of starfish development (1)

For each two students

_____ small test tube with sea urchin sperm
_____ small test tube with sea urchin eggs
prepared slides of:
_____   16-hour chick development (1)
_____   24-hour chick development (1)
live chick eggs incubated for:
_____   48 hours (1)
_____   96 hours (1)

LAB TOPIC 26

Animal Behavior

In this lab topic, students are required first to perform a short demonstration experiment (Experiment A of each exercise), then to work in teams to design and perform an additional experiment, choosing one of the options presented (Experiment B of each exercise). All materials in the Experiment A materials list should be available. You may choose to vary the materials for the Experiment B activities, depending on your own ideas and those of your students and the availability of animals. If possible, encourage independent ideas by supplying additional materials as requested. New in this edition, we have included a template that can be used to assist student teams in developing their proposals. Using a template will simplify evaluating their proposals and preparing the materials needed for their open-inquiry investigations.

For Each Four Students

Exercise 26.1, Experiment A
- 6 brine shrimp (*Artemia salina*)
- 1 large test tube (25 mm × 150 mm)
- 1 small finger bowl (approximately 11-cm culture dish)
- 1 piece (8½ in. × 11 in.) of black construction paper to use as a background
- 500 mL of salt water (1% NaCl) in flask

Exercise 26.1, Experiment B
- supplies from Experiment A
- 2 large test tubes (25 mm × 150 mm)
- piece of black cloth
- 4 rubber bands to hold cloth around the test tube
- lamp
- aluminum foil to direct light from lamp to test tube
- ice
- magnets
- rock salt crystals
- salt solutions of different concentrations
- dropper bottles of:
    5% sugar solution
    5% albumin solution
    5% acetic acid
    5% ammonium hydroxide

Exercise 26.2, Experiment A
- 10 terrestrial isopods: sow bug (*Oniscus asellus*) or pill bug (*Cylisticus convexus* can roll itself into a ball.)

- 2 large glass petri dishes (150 mm × 15 mm)
- 2 pieces of filter paper to fit petri dishes
- 1 squirt bottle of water

Exercise 26.2, Experiment B

- supplies from Experiment A
- 1 white enamel pan (10 in. × 15 in.)
- 2 wax pencils
- 1 manila folder or large card to cover the pan
- 500 mL of water in a beaker
- 1 piece (8½ in. × 11 in.) of black construction paper
- large pieces of black cloth
- 6 rubber bands

Exercise 26.3, Experiment A

- 1 male Siamese fighting fish (*Betta splendens*) in a 1–2-L, flat-sided fishbowl
- mirror
- watch or smartphone that displays seconds (each student should have one)

Exercise 26.3, Experiment B

- supplies from Experiment A
- colored pencils
- index cards
- brightly colored paper
- scissors
- wooden applicator sticks
- transparent tape
- fish of different species in fishbowl
- female Siamese fighting fish in a fishbowl

Exercise 26.4, Experiment A

- stereoscopic microscope
- fly vial with 2–3 virgin female fruit flies (*Drosophila melanogaster*)

  You can use wild type, but if flies with curly wings are available, use these for the females to facilitate easy identification of the females.

- vial with 2–3 male fruit flies with normal, wild-type wings
- petri dish (Optional; male and female flies can be placed in this before observing their behavior with the stereoscopic microscope.)

Exercise 26.4, Experiment B

- fly vial with 2–3 virgin females of an alternate species (other than *D. melanogaster*)
- fly vial with 2–3 males of an alternate species

  It is interesting to note that there are over 1500 described species of **Drosophila**! Here are just a few: *Drosophila endobranchia, Drosophila meridiana, Drosophila busckii, Drosophila pseudoobscura, Drosophila bifurca, Drosophila simulans, Drosophila lanaiensis, Drosophila funebris.* If members of your department or other colleges in the area work with fruit flies, ask if they have alternate species other than *D. melanogaster*.

Instructor's Desk

- projection technology (computer with digital projector). You may choose to show some of the videos suggested in the laboratory manual Student Media section.

Solution Preparation Notes

Salt Water (1% NaCl)

Add 1 g NaCl (sodium chloride, Carolina Biological Supply # 888880) to 100 mL DI water. Stir to mix.

For the following four solutions (sugar, acetic acid, ammonium hydroxide, and egg albumin), add a different color of food coloring to each solution. Place each colored solution in a dropper bottle. Students should carefully add the solutions (one at a time) to the surface of the water in the test tube with the shrimp. This allows students to see the test solution in the salt water. This facilitates observing the brine shrimp behavior (students can see if the shrimp swim toward or away from the colored solution).

5% Sugar Solution (5% Sucrose)

Add 5 g sucrose (Carolina Biological Supply # 892860) to 100 mL DI water. Stir and heat to mix if necessary.

5% Acetic Acid

Add 5 mL acetic acid (Carolina Biological Supply # 841290) to 100 mL DI water. Stir to mix. Remember to add acid to water, not the opposite.

5% Ammonium Hydroxide

Add 5 mL ammonium hydroxide (Carolina Biological Supply # 844010) to 100 mL DI water. Stir to mix.

5% Egg Albumin

Add 5 g powdered egg albumin (Carolina Biological Supply # 842251) to 100 mL DI water. Stir to mix.

Fish Water

Have aged tap water available for the fish. Allow about 5 L of tap water to sit overnight to prepare this water. Alternatively, use pond water.

Live/Prepared Materials

Brine shrimp and Siamese fighting fish are usually available in local pet stores, or they can be ordered from a biological supply house. Gently aerate the brine shrimp culture using a piece of aquarium tubing and an air stone. They live longer if kept at 15°C.

Pill bugs are common in warmer weather in most areas of the United States. Check for them in wood piles, under rotting logs, under flowerpots, and under rocks. They can also be ordered from Carolina Biological Supply, # 143082.

Order fruit flies from Carolina Biological Supply or another biological supply house if you do not have a local source. Order them to arrive 5 weeks before needed, and expand the cultures by crossing the flies 1 day, waiting for 3 days, and adding the parents to another set of bottles. Continue this at 3-day intervals for several transfers. Begin to collect virgin females and separate out males 2 weeks before the lab. See notes on collecting virgin female flies in Lab Topic 9. Female *Drosophila* should be virgins. Males should be several days old because young males emit inhibiting pheromones. One reference I have used indicates that males should also be virgins; however, another reference reports that experienced males more readily show mating behaviors. You may choose to try both virgin and experienced males. (Actually, this would be a good experiment for a student.) Keep the males and females separated in vials with adequate food.

Wild type *Drosophila melanogaster* (Carolina Biological Supply # 172100; curly wing variety # 172750)

Checklist of Materials

Equipment

For each four students

_____ stereoscopic microscope (1)
_____ large test tubes (3)
_____ small finger bowls (2)
_____ large glass petri dishes (2)
_____ filter paper to fit large petri dishes (2)
_____ medium-sized petri dish (1)
_____ mirror (1)
_____ white enamel pan (1)
_____ lamp (1)
_____ aluminum foil (1 roll)
_____ wax pencils (2)
_____ colored pencils (1 box)
_____ 3-in. × 5-in. index cards (10)
_____ watch or smartphone that displays seconds (each student)
_____ brightly colored paper
_____ scissors
_____ wooden applicator sticks
_____ transparent tape
_____ 8½-in. × 11-in. pieces of black construction paper (2)
_____ large pieces of black cloth (4)
_____ rubber bands (8)
_____ manila folder (1)

Instructor's Desk

_____ projection technology (computer with digital projector)

Live/Prepared Materials

For each four students

_____ brine shrimp, *Artemia salina* (6; with extras available)
_____ pill bugs, isopods (10; with extras available)
_____ male Siamese fighting fish, *Betta splendens,* in flat-sided fishbowl (1)
_____ female *Betta splendens* in fishbowl (1)
_____ fish of different species in fishbowls (various kinds)
_____ virgin female *Drosophila* with curly wings in vial (2–3; with extras available)
_____ male wild-type *Drosophila* in vial (2–3; with extras available)
_____ virgin females of alternate *Drosophila* species in vial (2–3; with extras available)
_____ male of alternate *Drosophila* species in vial (2–3; with extras available)

Solutions/Chemicals

For each four students

_____ salt water, 1% NaCl in 500-mL flask (500 mL)
dropper bottle of:
_____ 5% sugar solution (1)
_____ 5% albumin solution (1)
_____ 5% acetic acid (1)
_____ 5% ammonium hydroxide (1)
_____ squirt bottle of water (1)
_____ 500-mL beaker of water (1)
_____ ice
_____ magnets
_____ rock salt crystals
_____ salt solutions of different concentrations

For each class

_____ 24-hour-old tap water (5 L)

Animal Behavior Research Proposal

Team Name: **Team Members:**

Date: **Instructor:**

Question:

Hypothesis:

Prediction:

Summary of the Procedures:

Describe briefly the steps of your procedures, paying attention to the organisms, solutions, containers, equipment, and instrumentation that will be required. Consider the number of replicates, environmental conditions, and variables to be measured. As you develop your procedure, you may want to design a table for collecting data and copy to a USB drive to download on the computers in lab.

Materials:

List the materials that are required to implement your research. Include the organisms, glassware, solutions, tools, and equipment or instruments that you will need for your experiments. Include the numbers for each and other details that may be important.

LAB TOPIC 27

Ecology I: Terrestrial Ecology

In this lab, students work in teams of six to eight. Each team will sample a plot using the materials found in their field box. Within teams, each student will have specific responsibilities, as described below.

Exercise 27.1, Biotic Components

> Field Study A, two students
> Field Study B, two students
> Field Studies C, D, and E, two students
> Field Study F, students in Exercise 27.2 to complete this field study
> Field Study G, all students

Exercise 27.2, Abiotic Components, two students

Determine the number of teams, and prepare a field box containing all sampling equipment and instructions needed by the students. These can be grouped into smaller boxes or bags according to the field study. An instructor's box is also prepared according to the directions below.

We divide this lab into 2 weeks, doing our fieldwork the first week (Exercises 27.1 and 27.2) and our data analysis (Exercise 27.3) the next week. At the end of the exercise, we have each team present its data using a computer projector or overhead transparencies of Figures 27.7 and 27.8. Refer to the Teaching Plan, Order of the Lab, for suggestions for completing this lab in a single 3-hour lab or a 2-hour lab. Some materials must be set up in lab (for example, agar plates and Berlese-Tullgren funnels).

The lab preparator and instructor should discuss the *location of appropriate field sites* for this lab (omit this if you, like so many of us, wear both of these hats). The Teaching Plan includes suggestions for field studies, matters relating to *transportation of students*, and *identification of plants*. Although the lab is written for a forest ecosystem, the basic framework and exercises are adaptable to the ubiquitous weedy field. At the end of Lab Topic 25, an Optional Exercise is included for weedy fields, and an alternate organizational plan is included at the end of the Teaching Plan. If one of these options is selected, the preparation of field boxes should be adjusted accordingly.

Planning for Lab

1. Locate the field site.
2. Determine the mode of transportation and provide students with instructions (see Teaching Plan).
3. Reserve vans if necessary.

4. Visit the field site prior to lab and establish the points to be used for the center of the sampling plots. We install center stakes at these locations, then flag them with fluorescent survey tape for easy location. You can simply flag sites and let students install center stakes.
5. Place the min/max thermometer at the field site. Since these are expensive, we conceal them.
6. If expertise in plant identification is a concern, prepare a field guide specific for your study site. One inexpensive and efficient method is to collect examples of leaves from the most commonly observed plants in the sample sites. Use a photocopier to make black-and-white outline copies of each plant, and label each sheet. Compile an identification booklet using the expertise of botanists, ecologists, foresters, or landscapers.

For Each Student

- field notebook and pencil, Exercise 27.2, Field Study C (We have students supply their own.)

Exercise 27.3

- summary of all data sheets
- calculator

For Each Team

Exercise 27.1

- 2 Berlese-Tullgren funnels set up in lab (See Materials Preparation Notes.)
- light source for each funnel
- several stereoscopic microscopes set up in lab (used to identify organisms)
- 2 agar plates set up in lab
- min/max thermometer (Ben Meadows # 110135), Exercise 27.2, Field Study B

  Set the thermometer out in the plot 24 hours before lab. If all teams are sampling in the same general area, one min/max thermometer can be used for all teams.

- team field box (1 per team) (See below.)

Exercise 27.3

- computer for each team to complete data analysis
- Tables 27.3, 27.4, 27.5, 27.6, 27.9, 27.10, 27.11, 27.12, and 27.13 downloaded from masteringbiology.com
- overhead transparencies or scanned images of Figures 27.7, 27.8 (for final discussion in lab)

Field Box

Exercise 27.1, Field Studies A and B

- insect repellent
- clippers (hand pruners)
- 3 plot lines (See Materials Preparation Notes.)
- center post (¾–1-in. metal pipe)
- mallet
- DBH tape (Ben Meadows # 122480), or meter tape, (10 meters Carolina Biological Supply # 702636, 30 meters # 702637)

- index cards and 3–4 permanent markers in self-sealing plastic bag
- large plastic specimen bags and rubber bands
- calipers (FSB only) (Ben Meadows # 103334)
- plant ID booklet prepared for field site (photocopies of leaves)

Exercise 27.1, Field Study C

- circular 0.50-m^2 plot (See Materials Preparation Notes.)
- compass (REI # 890929) (Carolina Biological Supply # 758669, 758685)
- index cards and permanent marker
- large plastic specimen bags and rubber bands

Exercise 27.1, Field Study D

In addition to the items for Field Study C, which can be shared:

- thin plastic sheet (dry-cleaning bag)
- 6 pairs forceps
- 6 dissecting probes
- 4 vials with 70% propanol (We sometimes use rubbing alcohol.)
- labeling tape

Exercise 27.1, Field Study G

- binoculars

Exercise 27.2, Field Study A

- soil thermometer (Ben Meadows # 225976)
- soil auger/sampler (Ben Meadows # 221700)
- plastic self-sealing bags (gallon)
- trowel
- diagram of soil profile
- soils map of the area (available from local Soil Conservation Service or county extension agent)
- soils test kit with instructions (See Materials Preparation Notes.)

Exercise 27.2, Field Study B

- NOAA Climatological Data Sheets (Access the Weather Service data by zip code at http://w2.weather.gov/climate/local_data.php?wfo=ffc)
- sling psychrometer (with instructions and water bottle) (Ward's Biological Supply # 231181)
- light meter (with instructions) (Ward's Biological Supply # 145156, Extech makes several models available for several vendors.)
- 2–3 thermometers
- wind anemometer (with instructions) (Ben Meadows # 110950)
- min/max thermometer with directions (Ben Meadows # 6JF-110135)
- gun-style infrared thermometer (Ben Meadows # 192498)
- infrared thermometer with anemometer (optional; Ward's # 231258)

Exercise 27.2, Field Study C

- field notebook
- pencil
- USGS topographic map for study site

Instructor's Field Box

- first aid kit
- field guides (can be in team boxes if you have multiple copies)
- 8 specimen bags and rubber bands
- 2 clippers (hand pruners)
- 2 permanent markers
- 8 index cards

Instructor's Desk

- projection technology (computer with digital projector or document camera, or overhead projector)
- Download Tables 27.2, 27.3, 27.4, 27.5, 27.6, 27.9, 27.10, 27.11, 27.12, and 27.13 in Excel format from www.masteringbiology.com in Instructor Resources. Students can record their data and analyze the results.

Materials Preparation Notes

Most of the instruments can be ordered from Forestry Suppliers, Inc., Ben Meadows, Ward's, or Carolina Biological Supply.

Center Post

The pipe for the center post can be purchased from the plumbing or electrical department of a hardware or building supply store. The diameter of the pipe should accommodate the three clips used on the plot lines. Check this before having the pipe cut into sections. Our posts are approximately 3 ft long.

Plot Lines (3)

We use a heavy cord or rope with a chain clip ("dog leash clip") tied to one end and a tent stake tied to the other. The clip size must allow three lines to be attached to the center post. Check this before leaving the hardware store! The knots are wrapped and secured with duct tape. The lines should be 5.64 m long, flagged with bright labeling or surveyor's tape 4 m out from the chain clip end. Refer to Figure 27.3.

Circular 0.50-m² Plot

These sampling plots were made by our physical plant from galvanized sheet metal that has been cut and welded together. File the edges smooth and cover with duct tape to prevent sharp edges. These are 80 cm in diameter.

Berlese-Tullgren Funnels

These can be homemade using a 2-L soft drink bottle, a mesh screen or drywall joint tape, a small bag with preservative, and a light above. Cut the bottle in half and invert the top portion. Attach the plastic bag to the mouth of the top. Rest the top of the bottle inside the bottom. Position two pieces of drywall joint tape, adhesive side down (15 cm each), in a cross shape covering the opening of the inverted top. (See Figure 27.5 in the lab manual.) Funnels may be purchased (Carolina Biological Supply # 654148). Set up the funnels in the laboratory for students to place their samples when they return from their field sites. Use a 50-W bulb as a light source and 70% EtOH to collect the insects.

Agar Plates

Sterile nutrient agar plates can be purchased from a biological supply house or made in the lab if an autoclave is available. These, too, must be ready for students to use when they return from their field sites. If you will make your own, refer to the instructions in Lab Topic 13, Bacteriology.

Soil Test Kit

Soils collected may be tested for various components: LaMotte soil test kit (Ben Meadows # 221245) and tests for pH, nitrogen, phosphorus, and potassium. The soil texture unit, Ben Meadows # 224255, classifies soil by sand-silt-clay composition. Determine the appropriate soil test for your field site before ordering.

Reference Materials

- Obtain NOAA data sheets from your local weather station. Try the Weather Service data by zip code at http://w2.weather.gov/climate/local_data.php?wfo=ffc.
- To find and order USGS topographic maps of the study site, see https://www.usgs.gov/products/maps/topo-maps
- You should be able to locate your study site using Google Earth.
- *Soil Biology Primer* [online]. Available: http://soils.usda.gov/sqi/concepts/soil_biology/biology.html
- EPA Ecosystems Web page, Terrestrial and Aquatic Ecosystems, Watersheds in your area of the United States: http://water.epa.gov/type/watersheds/index.cfm
- Field guides will be valuable for both students and the instructor. Choose several from the following list or purchase guides specific for your area. We have included a few that should be available for various regions. In Georgia, the Forestry Commission has an excellent small tree guide (available free for teachers and students) that includes all the major trees. Contact the regional or local offices of the U.S. Forest Service and the Forestry Commission or equivalent for your state. The County Extension Service can also be of assistance.

Field Guides for Identification of Organisms

Richard L. Boyce. April 2005, posting date. Life Under Your Feet: Measuring Soil Invertebrate Diversity. *Teaching Issues and Experiments in Ecology*, Vol. 3: Experiment #1 [online]. http://tiee.ecoed.net/vol/v3/experiments/soil/abstract.html. Downloadable soil invertebrate key accessed at http://tiee.ecoed.net/vol/v3/experiments/soil/downloads.html.

Elias, T. 1987. *The Complete Trees of North America*. New York: Random House Publishing., Van Nostrand Reinhold.

Kirkman, L.K., C.L. Brown, and D.J. Leopold. 2007. *Native Trees of the Southeast*. Portland: Timber Press.

Kwik-Key to Soil-Dwelling Invertebrates: http://www.cals.ncsu.edu/course/ent525/soil/kwikey1.html

Pimentel, R. A. 1967. *Invertebrate Identification Manual.* New York: Reinhold.

Smith, J. P. 1981. *A Key to the Genera of Grasses of the Conterminous United States.* Eureka, CA: Mad River Press.

Peterson Field Guides

The series of field guides includes all major ecosystems, plants, animals, and fungi by major taxa and region. For a list of all the guides and the latest editions, go to the Houghton Mifflin Books website: http://www.houghtonmifflinbooks.com/peterson/

National Audubon Society Field Guides and Regional Guides

The Audubon Field Guides cover major taxonomic groups, animals, plants, fungi, and more. In addition Audubon Regional Guides cover the major ecosystems by region and then highlight important plants and animals in those ecosystems and regions. Random House now includes the publisher Knopf. The series can be reviewed at: http://knopfdoubleday.com/book/119969/national-audubon-society-field-guide-to-north-american-mushrooms/

In addition, field guides to Birds, Mammals, Wildflowers, and Trees can be downloaded as apps: http://www.audubonguides.com/field-guides/birds-mammals-wildflowers-trees-north-america.html

Macmillan Field Guides

Bull, J. L. 1989. *Birds of North America: Western Region.* New York: Collier Macmillan.

Mohlenbrock, R. H. 1987. *A Quick Identification Guide to the Wildflowers of North America.* New York: Macmillan.

Mohlenbrock, R. H. 1987. *Trees: A Quick Reference Guide to Trees of North America.* New York: Macmillan.

Other Field Guides and Apps

Discover Life Nature ID Guides:
http://www.discoverlife.org/mp/20q

Encyclopedia of Life Field Guides—find or create your own using the tools and apps:
http://fieldguides.eol.org/

Checklist of Materials

Supplies

For each student

_____ field notebook and pencil (1)
_____ summary of all data sheets (1)
_____ calculator (1)

Field Boxes

For each student

_____ forceps (1)
_____ dissecting probes (1)

For each team

_____ insect repellent (1 container)
_____ clippers (1)
_____ plot lines (3)
_____ center post (1)
_____ mallet (1)
_____ DBH or meter tape (1)
_____ index cards and 3–4 permanent markers in self-sealing bag (1)
_____ plastic specimen bags and rubber bands (3 each)
_____ calipers (1)
_____ circular 0.50-m^2 plot (1)
_____ compass (1)
_____ thin plastic sheet (dry-cleaning bag) (1)
_____ vials of 70% alcohol (4)
_____ labeling tape, roll (1)
_____ binoculars (1)
_____ soil thermometer (1)
_____ soil auger (1)
_____ plastic self-sealing gallon bags (1 box)
_____ trowel (1)
_____ diagram of soil profile (1)
_____ soils map of the area (1)
_____ soil test kit with instructions (1)
_____ NOAA Climatological Data Sheets (1)
_____ sling psychrometer with instructions and water bottle (1)
_____ light meter with instructions (1)
_____ thermometers (2–3)
_____ wind anemometer with instructions (1)
_____ infrared thermometer with anemometer (optional)
_____ field site ID booklet (optional) (2)

Instructor's Field Box

_____ first aid kit (1)
_____ plastic specimen bags and rubber bands (8 each)
_____ field guides (assortment)
_____ clippers (2)
_____ permanent markers (2)
_____ index cards (8)

Instructor's Desk

_____ projection technology (computer with digital projector or document camera, or overhead projector)
_____ Tables 27.2, 27.3, 27.4, 27.5, 27.6, 27.9, 27.10, 27.11, 27.12, and 27.13 downloaded in Excel format from www.masteringbiology.com
_____ USB drive

Setup in Lab

_____ Berlese-Tullgren funnels with light source (2)
_____ agar plates (2)
_____ scanned images or overhead transparencies of Figures 27.7, 27.8 (1 each)
_____ computer with tables downloaded in Excel format

Setup in Plots 24 Hours Before Lab

_____ min/max thermometer (1)

Ecology II:
Computer Simulations of a Pond Ecosystem

The 2002 version of *Environmental Decision Making* is used in this lab topic. *Environmental Decision Making* is now available for free and can be downloaded from the BioQUEST Library Online (http://bioquest.org/BQLibrary/library_result.php). See the preparation notes on software requirements.

Ideally, this lab would be taught in a laboratory with enough computers for each three or four students or in a computer lab with similar facilities. However, this lab can be organized to introduce students in small groups of six to eight to the investigation and modeling software at staggered times. Then you can have the students complete the simulations outside of lab time using computer facilities on campus. Ideally, using an interactive whiteboard or projector, the instructor will introduce the basic components of the model and then assist as the students begin the first investigations. The students will then work at their own pace designing their investigations and reporting their results at the end of the laboratory. Consult with the instructor and determine the computer facilities available at your institution. The support staff at the BioQUEST office are terrific at solving problems and supporting teaching using their programs. For information, begin at their website—www.bioquest.org.

Note that the Extend LT application must be downloaded to create and use the models in Environmental Decision Making. Extend LT is compatible with current Windows operating systems; however, at this time, Extend will not work with Apple operating systems newer than 2013. For additional information contact BioQUEST. Other software is available to construct a model, but it generally does not incorporate all the features of this program. See the References section in the laboratory manual for other models that are available. Note that we have not used these models with our students.

For Each Student

- USB drive (students supply their own)

For Each Four Students

- computer software (MAC and PC compatible)

  Odum, E., H. Odum, and N. Peterson. 2001. *Environmental Decision Making.* The BioQUEST Library, Vol. VI. Jungck, J., and V. Vaughan (Eds.). San Diego: Harcourt/ Academic Press.

  Download the software for free from the BioQUEST Library Online at http:// bioquest.org/BQLibrary/library_result.php.

- computer hardware

Macintosh Modules

Macintosh: with at least 8 megabytes of RAM (16 MB recommended), running system 7.6.1 or higher. The programs will not work with operating systems newer than 2013. See note above.

PC Modules

- Windows 95 or later
- at least 8 megabytes of RAM

Instructor's Desk

- projection technology (computer with digital projector or document camera, or overhead projector)
- computer with software downloaded
- USB drive
- Select a video to introduce Experiment C about Asian carp. Two examples:
  http://www.youtube.com/watch?v=ZpZ7smai2p8
  http://www.invasivespeciesinfo.gov/aquatics/asiancarp.shtml#.UOJhekJNGfQ

Checklist of Materials

Equipment

For each student

_____ USB drive (students supply their own)

For each four students

_____ computer with software downloaded (1)

Instructor's Desk

_____ projection technology (computer with digital projector or document camera, or overhead projector)
_____ computer with software downloaded
_____ USB drive

Vendor Addresses

BarnDoor Lighting Outfitters
232 Branford Road
North Branford, CT 06471
1-203-208-0615
FAX 1-203-208-0634
info@barndoorlighting.com

Baxter Diagnostics, Inc.
Scientific Products Division
1430 Waukegan Road
McGaw Park, IL 60085-6787
Toll-free numbers by state
www.baxter.com

Ben Meadows Co.
3589 Broad Street
Atlanta (Chamblee), GA 30341
1-800-241-6401
FAX: 1-800-628-2068
www.benmeadows.com

Carolina Biological Supply
Burlington, NC 27215
1-800-334-5551
FAX: 1-800-222-7112
carolina@carolina.com
www.carolina.com

Cleveland Scientific
P.O. Box 300
Bath, OH 44210
1-800-952-7315
FAX: 1-330-666-2240
www.clevelandscientific.com

Connecticut Valley Biological Supply Co.
P.O. Box 326
82 Valley Road
Southhampton, MA 01073
1-800-628-7748
FAX: 1-800-355-6813
info@ctvalleybio.com
www.ctvalleybio.com

Delta Biologicals
P.O. Box 26666
Tucson, AZ 85726-6666
1-800-821-2502
FAX: 1-520-745-7888
www.deltabio.com

Difco Laboratories is now owned by
Becton, Dickinson and Company (BD
Diagnostic Systems). www.bd.com
Also check other distributors for Difco
products (e.g., Fisher Scientific).

Edmund Scientific Company
60 Pearce Ave.
Tonawanda, NY 14150
1-800-728-6999
www.scientificsonline.com

EDVOTEK, Inc.
1121 5th Street NW
Washington, DC 20001
1-800-338-6835
FAX: 1-800-202-370-1501
info@edvotek.com
www.edvotek.com

Fisher Scientific
2000 Park Lane Dr.
Pittsburgh, PA 15275
1-800-766-7000
FAX: 1-800-926-1166
www.fishersci.com

Forestry Suppliers, Inc.
P.O. Box 8397
Jackson, MS 39284-8397
1-800-647-5368
FAX: 1-800-543-4203
www.forestry-suppliers.com

FOTODYNE, Inc.
950 Walnut Ridge Drive
Hartland, WI 53029
1-262-369-7000
1-800-362-3686 toll-free
FAX 262-369-7017
www.fotodyne.com

Geological Enterprises
P.O. Box 996
Ardmore, OK 73402
1-580-223-8537
geoent@ardmore.com
www.geologicalenterprises.com

Gulf Specimen
(for living marine invertebrates)
P.O. Box 237
222 Clark Drive
Panacea, FL 32346
1-850-984-5297
FAX: 1-850-984-5333
www.gulfspecimen.org
Web page includes information
on maintaining sea urchins and
their embryology.

Marine Biological Laboratory
Aquatic Resources Division
7 MBL Street
Woods Hole, MA 02543
1-508-289-7375
www.mbl.edu
To check availability of specific organisms, e-mail specimens@MBL.edu.

MedSuppliesShop
1-800-544-9104
http://www.medsuppliesshop.com/

Modern Biology, Inc.
3710 East 700 Spitj
Lafayette, IN 47909
1-800-773-6544
FAX 765-523-3397
www.modernbiol.com

New England BioGroup
P.O. Box 1231
Atkinson, NH 03811
1-800-779-1016
FAX: 1-617-334-0055
info@nebiogroup.com

New England BioLabs, Inc.
32 Tozer Road
Beverly, MA 01915-5599
1-800-632-5227
FAX: 1-800-632-7440
info@neb.com
orders@neb.com
www.neb.com

REI (Recreational Equipment Inc.)
Many retail stores available. Check your
local listing. www.rei.com

Sigma-Aldrich Chemical Company
P.O. Box 14508
St. Louis, MO 63178-9916
1-800-325-3010
FAX: 1-800-325-5052
www.sigma-aldrich.com

Thermo Scientific
Thermo Fisher Scientific Inc.
81 Wyman Street
Waltham, MA 02454
1-800-678-5599
FAX: 1-781-622-1207
www.thermoscientific.com

Thomas Scientific
P.O. Box 99
Swedesboro, NJ 08085
1-856-467-2000
Customer Service: 800-345-2100
www.thomassci.com/

Triarch Incorporated
P.O. Box 98
Ripon, WI 54971
1-800-848-0810
FAX: 1-888-848-0810
www.triarchmicroslides.com

USA Scientific
P.O. Box 3565
Ocala, FL 34487
1-800-522-8477
FAX: 1-352-351-2057
www.usascientific.com

Vernier Software & Technology
13979 SW Millikan Way
Beaverton, OR 97005
1-888-837-6437
Fax 503-277-2440
Email info@vernier.com
www.vernier.com

VWR Scientific
1310 Goshen Parkway
West Chester, PA 19380
1-800-932-5000 (toll free # to order from
the VWR office nearest you)
www.vwr.com

Ward's Natural Science Establishment, Inc.
5100 W. Henrietta Road
P.O. Box 92912
Rochester, NY 14692-9012
1-800-962-2660
FAX: 1-800-635-8439
www.wardsci.com